How I Multiplied
My Income and Happiness
in Selling

Also by Frank Bettger

_How I Raised Myself
from Failure to Success
in Selling_

How I
Multiplied My Income
and Happiness
in Selling

by
Frank Bettger

Prentice-Hall, Inc.
Englewood Cliffs, N. J.

How I Multiplied My Income and Happiness in Selling
by Frank Bettger
Copyright ©1982, 1954 by Prentice Hall, Inc.
Copyright under International and
Pan American Copyright Conventions
Address inquiries to Prentice-Hall, Inc.,
Englewood Cliffs, N.J. 07632
Printed in the United States of America
Prentice-Hall International, Inc., London
Prentice-Hall of Australia, Pty. Ltd., Sydney
Prentice-Hall of Canada, Ltd., Toronto
Prentice-Hall of India Private Ltd., New Delhi
Prentice-Hall of Japan, Inc., Tokyo
Prentice-Hall of Southeast Asia Pte. Ltd., Singapore
Whitehall Books Limited, Wellington, New Zealand

15   14   13   12   11   10

Library of Congress Cataloging in Publication Data

Bettger, Frank.
How I multiplied my income and happiness in selling.
Includes index.
1. Selling   I. Title.
HF5438.25.B47   1982   658.8'5   81-19911
ISBN 0-13-423962-8   AACR2
ISBN 0-13-423954-7 (PBK.)

Why I Wrote This Book

ONE DAY in the summer of 1949, I took the train to New York from my home in Wynnewood, Pa., near Philadelphia. Under my arm I carried the manuscript of a book which had taken me five years to write. I hoped somebody would be willing to publish it.

A few months later, when that book, *How I Raised Myself from Failure to Success in Selling,* jumped to the "big ten" on the national best-seller lists, right along with best-selling fiction, I was dumbfounded! It all seemed so fantastic!

I was even more astounded when letters began pouring in, thanking me for writing the book . . . letters from people all over the United States and Canada, asking me for more details about my experiences in selling.

I had devoted the book largely to my principles, techniques, and my philosophy of selling. Now, they wanted to know precisely how I *applied* them. They wanted my actual sales procedure: sales talks, word for word. Complete details of my prospecting methods. Copies of proposals. Questionnaires. My "13 Weeks' Self-Organizer."

It was a tremendous compliment to me . . . the guy who once thought of himself as the "world's greatest failure."

For a long while, I attempted to reply to everybody—answer their questions and send them the material they asked for. But when the book was published in twelve foreign languages, and mail began coming in from all over the world . . . I was snowed under!

Letters piled up, and I got so far behind in my correspondence that it became a great burden to me.

There was no time left for my family.

... Then one day, it dawned on me what had been going on! These questions and problems I had been trying to answer individually by mail had been driving me on to write another book—*this book!*

I wouldn't want to give anyone the impression that this book has been written to order. It has grown and developed out of the records and files I've kept for thirty-six years. It has grown out of talks I have made in the past twelve years to more than 150,000 salesmen and executives in 214 cities from Portland, Ore., to Miami, Fla. And it has sprung from the many personal interviews and conversations I have enjoyed with these wonderful people ... wherever I have gone.

I have discovered what every salesman would love to do, more than anything else—would almost give his right arm to do—is:

> "Go right out on the 'firing line' with some of the top salesmen, and *see* them actually perform! *Hear* exactly what they say, and what they do! ... The 'know how' and the 'show-how'!"

So, that's exactly what I have tried to produce in this book. Actual interviews. Actual prospecting methods. Actual preparation. And actual self-organization.

... In my first book, I tried to write as though you were sitting right alongside of me while I was talking with you. This book, I have tried to write just as though you and I were partners, out selling together. You'll go along with me every step of the way this time! I hope you like it.

Contents

Author's Preface—Why I Wrote This Book . . . vii

PART ONE

OUT OF THE DEPTHS OF FAILURE

1. I Had Two Strikes on Me When I Broke into Selling   1

2. A $25,000 Idea That Started Me on the Road to Success   8

3. A Mathematical Discovery That Raised Me from Ninety-second to First Place in My Company . . 14

4. The Biggest Problem of All and How I Licked It . 19

SUMMARY AND MAGIC PHRASES—Part One . . . 28
    Little Things That Made Me a Better Salesman—
    No. 1: How I Learned to Lick the Depression . . 31

PART TWO

MY ENTIRE SELLING PROCESS—STEP BY STEP

5. The Most Difficult Step in the Sale and How I Handle It 37

6. How I Get All the Facts and Prepare for the Selling Interview 42

7. The Selling Interview 48

8. An Invaluable Lesson on Closing I Learned from an "Old-timer" 57

9. How Questions Converted a Skeptic into an Enthusiastic Buyer 59

10. Analysis of the Basic Sales Principles Used in Making That Sale 66
   Little Things That Made Me a Better Salesman— No. 2: An Idea I Learned in Baseball That I Have Used Every Day in Selling . . . 70

PART THREE

THE MOST PROFOUND SECRET OF SUCCESSFUL SELLING, AND HOW I LEARNED TO APPLY IT

11. The One Big Secret of Success 75

12. Applying This Principle Raised Them from Small Jobbers to Big Construction Engineers . . . 78

13. His Chief Objection Was a Buying Signal! . . 82

14. How I Learned to Get Faster and More Favorable Action from My Company 86

15. The Deal Before the Deal 89

16. I Lost the Sale, But Gained Something Far More Valuable Than the Commission I Would Have Made 93

17. A Magic Phrase That Helps Men Raise Their Sights 97

18. I Love to Deliver Rated Policies 102

19. How I Handle the Sale When One or More Partners Are Rejected 108

20. One of the Best Closing Tools I Have in My Kit . 115

SUMMARY—Part Three 118
*Little Things That Made Me a Better Salesman—
No. 3: After I Did This I Began to Sell As I Never
Sold Before* 119

PART FOUR

THE WORLD'S GREATEST CLOSER OF SALES!

21. The One Big Secret of Closing Sales I Learned from
a Master Salesman 125

22. A Powerful, Motivating Story 128

23. The Felix Isman Story 132

24. This Story Helps Me Get a Check with the Order 134

25. How to Make It Easy for Young Husbands and
Wives to Buy 138

26. Bring On Your Witnesses 142

27. The Profits from This Story Founded a Great University and Put Thousands of Young Men Through
College 148

SUMMARY—Part Four 150
*Little Things That Made Me a Better Salesman—
No. 4: How "Daddy's Little Girl" Closes Many Sales
for Me* 151

PART FIVE

AN EXCITING NEW FIELD OF BUSINESS THAT PUT ME INTO THE "BIG LEAGUES"

28. I Became a Bird Dog for One of the Nation's Greatest Salesmen 155

29. The Secret of How I Made One of My Biggest Sales 161

30. An Amazing Story That Has Helped Me Close Many Big Sales 168

31. He Wanted to Drop $25,000, But This Idea Sold Him $150,000 More 174

32. They Weren't Interested, Until These Ideas Made Them Want to Buy 183

33. Sharpshooting for the Right Key Man . . . 195

34. He Wouldn't Talk to Insurance Salesmen, But I Sold Him $137,500 198

Benjamin Franklin's Recommendation on Business Agreements 205

Little Things That Made Me a Better Salesman— No. 5: How I Conquered Fear and Developed Courage and Self-Confidence Rapidly . . . 206

PART SIX

WHY SHOULD YOU DO SOMETHING FOR NOTHING?

35. This Job Cost Me More Time and Energy Than I Calculated 211

36. "The Hell with It!" 216

37. "Bread Cast Upon the Waters . . ." . . . 221

Little Things That Made Me a Better Salesman— No. 6: The Dollars and Cents Value of a Call . . 225

PART SEVEN

IF YOU WERE MY OWN BROTHER . . .

38. From Bankrupt to Million Dollar Producer Within One Year 229

39. If You Were My Own Brother, I Would Say to You
What I Am Going to Say to You Now 233

FRANK BETTGER'S *13 WEEKS' SELF-
ORGANIZER* 237

CONFIDENTIAL QUESTIONNAIRES . . . 307

INDEX 309

PART ONE

Out of the Depths of Failure

1.

I Had Two Strikes on Me
When I Broke into Selling

I AM GOING to begin this book by telling about one of my experiences in baseball. You may think it doesn't have anything to do with selling, but it has. Just keep reading. . . .

I was a National League ballplayer, holding down the "hot corner" for the St. Louis Cardinals. I had worked my way up from the bush leagues. Now, I was rubbing elbows with some of those great players I had read about for years—players I had never even hoped to know—yet here I was on the same team with them!

It all seemed like a dream come true. Every day for two years, I was floating on air!

Then suddenly, without warning, the dream *exploded!* Playing a game one day in Chicago, I threw the ball, something snapped in my shoulder—and the dream was over. . . .

I looked in the mirror: "Yesterday a hero. Today a bum! A bum with a glass arm." A bad accident had changed me in a few seconds from a big league ballplayer to just another dub looking for a job.

I had two strikes on me when I returned home to Philadelphia. No education, no business training, no money—and the rent overdue! At the time, it was a great tragedy to me.

Then I remembered something an old man said to me one time. He said, "Frank, if you ever get out of work, go get a job —even if it's digging ditches. *Then,* look for a better one." . . . So I managed to get a job as a collector for George Kelly's in-

1

stallment furniture concern, 606 Market Street. And for two years, I made my living riding around the streets of Philadelphia on a bicycle, collecting installments—a dollar down and the balance in "uneasy" weekly payments.

This was pretty far removed from that "hero stuff" I'd gotten used to. The applause was all gone now. . . .

One day, as I rode along, I heard someone yell, "Frank . . . Frank Bettger!" I looked back, and there was Charlie Miller, an old baseball friend. I was so ashamed I felt like ducking up an alley. I didn't want anybody to know I had to make my living on a bicycle. But Charlie was waiting, so I went back.

It surprised me how well dressed and prosperous he looked. I was amazed how well he talked! This was a far different man from the Charlie Miller I had known. The last time I had seen him he was a "park sparrow." Just a bum in the park who wanted to be a ballplayer.

"Frank," he said, "I finally got wise and realized I didn't have what it took to be a ballplayer. So I got it out of my head, and decided I was going to try to make something of myself. *I'm in the life insurance business now!*"

Seeing what Charlie Miller had been able to do encouraged me. I thought, "If *he* could do it, why couldn't *I* do it?" . . . For days, I couldn't get Charlie Miller out of my mind.

Shortly afterward, I was given an emergency call to make at a home where some furniture had been delivered C.O.D. the day before, but the driver had been unable to collect the money. I rode right out there on my bike, expecting to have some trouble—but the man of the house came to the door, invited me into the living room, and handed me the cash covering the entire bill. He said, "You've saved me a trip into town. I was coming into the store this morning to pay it myself."

I thanked him, and we chatted a couple of minutes. He came to the front door with me as I left. I jumped on my bike and started off when I heard him calling me. He asked if I wouldn't come back in the house for just a minute.

I was curious as we sat down in the living room again. He said, "You look like too good a man to be doing work like this.

Are you married?" I nodded "Yes." "Do you have any children?" "One baby boy," I answered. "Would you mind telling me how much money you make?" he asked in a kindly way. "$18 a week," I replied.

. . . The following afternoon I met him in his office at two o'clock. He was assistant manager of a branch office of one of the largest life insurance companies. He introduced me to the manager.

That manager was the biggest talker I ever heard in all my life. Within one hour, he had me so completely sold on going into the life insurance business, I could hardly wait until he signed me up. But he *kept on* talking, and an hour later I began to have some doubts whether I did want to try the business. It was in the middle of winter, and later it got pitch dark outside, but he never stopped to take a breath. At six o'clock he was still going strong, but I had made up my mind that if I ever got out of that office he'd never see me again. And to my knowledge he never has!

Some days later, I recalled that the chairman of the athletic committee of Swarthmore College, where I had helped coach baseball for a few weeks the previous spring, was Secretary of the Fidelity Mutual Life Insurance Company. His name was Charles G. Hodge. I decided to go in and ask his advice about my chances of selling insurance.

Two weeks later I was in the business!

On a Monday morning, I left the house wearing my Sunday suit. It seemed strange to be starting off to work without my bike. I was a Life Insurance Salesman! I'll never forget the date. It was February 15, 1916 . . . my birthday! I was twenty-eight years old.

But I wasn't happy. I was scared! Frankly, I didn't expect to make good. My only hope was that it might get me around among other businesses and lead to something else that I *could* do. Anything where I wouldn't have to make my living on a bicycle.

My worst shock right in the beginning was that I was able to make up a list of *only thirty-seven* names: people I knew who I thought could afford to buy life insurance. I had been away from Philadelphia so much for several years, playing ball, I had lost contact with most of my friends. Only a few of them had the kind of job that would allow them to buy more than "burial insurance." That's all I had myself.

Those thirty-seven calls I lined up in territorial order. The first call was on an old friend named Warren Moss. I had gone to James G. Blaine Grammar School with him. He had become successful as a builder of homes. Being successful, I was afraid maybe he'd give me a fast "brush-off."

It was pouring rain as I opened the street door of his office. Two older men pushed by me as they were leaving, raising their umbrellas. There stood Warren Moss in the front office, back of a high counter. It had been years since I had seen him. He relieved my tension immediately with a big, warmhearted smile as he called out, "Frank Bettger! What in the world are you doing here?"

"I'm selling life insurance," I replied, as I tried to look natural and return his grand smile.

"Selling *life insurance!*" he exclaimed in surprise. "How long have you been doing that?"

"Just started," I grinned. *"You* are my first call."

"For heaven's sake, imagine that!" He looked at me as though he couldn't believe it. "Ralph!" he yelled to someone in the back room. A face appeared to see what had happened. It was Warren's younger brother. "You remember Frank Bettger, don't you? He went to Blaine School with us."

"Sure," smiled Ralph.

"What do you think Frank Bettger is doing?" Warren asked.

"I can't imagine," he grinned.

"He's just starting in the life insurance business and this is his *first call!*"

Ralph couldn't have looked more surprised.

"What's so amazing about *me* going into the life insurance business?" I asked.

"Did you notice those two men who just went out?" asked Warren.

"Yes."

"Well," laughed Warren, "one of them was a life insurance salesman with the Provident Mutual; the other was the doctor who examined Ralph for $10,000. If you had only come in here a few days sooner, we would have given the business to you!"

I must have looked sick, because both Warren and Ralph acted so sorry for me.

All the rest of that week, I brooded over this "bad break."

. . . The following Saturday afternoon, I stood on the corner of 4th and Vine Streets. It was 1:20 P.M. I was tired and hungry and I didn't feel as though I could afford to buy any lunch. I was *licked*. I had called on thirty-six out of the thirty-seven names on my list and the only thing I got was discouragement. Some of those old friends had actually been cruel. *"Why* did I have to pick out a business like this?" I asked myself.

There was just one more name on my list—another old friend named Harry Schmidt. "What's the use of going to see him?" I thought. "It will be the same thing, and I just can't take any more."

Then that small voice whispered in my ear: "Now look! It's only half a block away, and he won't be in on Saturday afternoon. Anyhow, you'll have the satisfaction of knowing you made every one of these thirty-seven calls before you quit!"

So, with the hope that he wouldn't be in, I walked down to his office. I was surprised to see a fine-looking building that ran all the way back to a small street in the rear. The big sign outside read:

HENRY SCHMIDT & BRO.

MANUFACTURERS OF HIGH GRADE PAPER-BOXES

It looked quiet around there. I was hoping the place was closed, but the front door opened. Inside, I could see that all the office help had gone. Just then . . . out walked my friend, Harry Schmidt!

"Hello, Frank," said he, recognizing me immediately. "What are you doing down here?" he asked as he shook hands with me.

"I came down to see *you,* Harry," I said.

"Come on back," he invited as he walked back into his own office. "Sit down, Frank. What are you doing now?"

"I'm selling life insurance," I answered, still scared.

"Oh, is that so. I've got a couple of policies in the Provident Mutual. Is that a good company?"

I had heard of the Provident Mutual, but I didn't know anything about them. I said, "Yes, that's a good company."

"Take a look at these," he said as he opened the office safe. "I think they cost too much money. What kind of policies are they?"

Well, I didn't know much about insurance, but even that was about 100 per cent more than Harry Schmidt knew! They were two $1,000, Fifteen Year Endowment policies. The annual premiums amounted to about $65 each. Luckily I did know what an endowment meant.

He said, "Aren't those premiums awful high?"

"Yes," I agreed, "they are high. Endowment policies are always high."

"What could you sell me $2,000 for, Frank?"

I pulled out my ratebook and saw that Twenty Payment Life at Age 27 would be only $34 per thousand. So I said, "$68, Harry."

He added $68 to the $130 he was already paying and said, "Go ahead and write me up for another $2,000."

I had sold my first policy!

... At the time, Harry Schmidt had no idea how much that meant to me. I was almost too excited to write the application. When he handed me his check for the annual premium, I was so grateful I could have kissed him!

That was thirty-seven years ago almost to the day that I am writing these lines. That policy, the first I ever wrote, is still in force—paid up, of course. Over the years, I placed several more with Harry Schmidt in much larger amounts. One, I sold to Henry Schmidt & Bro. for $150,000 on his life after Harry became president. I am going to tell about that sale later, but no sale I ever made was as important to me as this *first* one. It restored my courage and gave me the confidence to go on. In fact, I've often thought I probably wouldn't have stayed in the business if I hadn't *gone on,* that Saturday afternoon, and made that *one more call.*

2.

*A $25,000 Idea That Started Me
on the Road to Success*

EIGHT YEARS as a professional baseball player seemed to make me unfit for anything like selling life insurance. Hardly a day passed during that first year that I didn't think seriously of quitting. In fact, after ten months, I *had* to quit. (Confidentially, the company cut off my drawing account!) For several days I walked the streets answering want ads for a job, but with my lack of education and business experience, nobody wanted me.

I tried to get my old job back with George Kelly's, collecting on a bicycle at $18 a week—but even Kelly's turned me down cold.

I was not only discouraged. I was in the depths of despair.

. . . Then, if you read my book, *From Failure to Success in Selling,* or saw my film, you may recall how one morning I dropped into the insurance company office to pick up a couple of personal things I happened to leave in my desk. An agency meeting was going on at the time, and quite by accident I heard the president of the company, Walter LeMar Talbot, utter one sentence that has had a profound and lasting effect on my life for the past thirty-seven years. *That one sentence was this:*

Gentlemen, after all, this business of selling narrows down to one thing—just *one* thing . . . seeing the people! Show me any man of ordinary ability who will go out and earnestly tell his story to four or five people

8

every day, and I will show you a man who just can't help making good!

That one sentence put me back into the business!

During the next ten weeks, I sold more life insurance than I had been able to sell in the entire previous ten months! It wasn't much, but it proved to me that Mr. Talbot knew what he was talking about. I *could* sell!

It wasn't long, however, before I dropped back into my old habits, failing to make the calls. . . .

In baseball, they say *"you can't hit 'em if you don't see 'em."* At the rate I was "seeing 'em," the Fidelity would soon be trading me in for a broken bat!

One day I received a statement from the company. My debit balance was $478! *That shook me awake!* On a Saturday afternoon I took myself back to the office, locked myself in a little conference room and for three hours sat there having it out with myself: "What's the matter with me? Just what is wrong?" Finally, I remembered an article I had read in a magazine a few weeks before—it was so inspiring, I had torn it out and saved it. I went to my desk. It was still in the bottom drawer. . . .

A $25,000 Idea

One day an efficiency expert named Ivy Lee was interviewing Charles Schwab, president of Bethlehem Steel Company. Lee outlined his organization's service to Schwab, and ended by saying: "With our service, you'll know how to manage better."

"Hell," said Schwab, "I'm not managing as well now as I know how to. What we need is not more 'knowing,' but more 'doing'; not knowledge, but *action!* If you can give us something to pep us up to do the things we *already know we ought to do,* I'll gladly listen to you and pay you anything you ask!"

"Fine," answered Lee. "I can give you something in twenty minutes that will step up your action and doing at least 50%."

"Okay," said Schwab, "let's have it. I've got just about that much time before I leave to catch a train."

Time Management

Lee handed Mr. Schwab a blank note sheet from his pocket and said: "Write on this paper the six most important tasks you have to do tomorrow." That took about three minutes. "Now," said Lee, "number them in the order of their importance." Schwab took five minutes for that. "Now," said Lee, "put this paper in your pocket and the first thing tomorrow morning look at item one and start working on it until it is finished. Then tackle item two in the same way; then item three, and so on. Do this until quitting time. Don't be concerned if you have only finished one or two. You'll be working on the most important ones. The others can wait. If you can't finish them all by this method, you couldn't have with any other method either; and without some system, you'd probably not even have decided which was the most important.

"Do this every working day. After you've convinced yourself of the worth of this system, have your men try it. Try it as long as you wish, and then send me a check for what you think it is worth."

The whole interview lasted about thirty minutes. In a few weeks Schwab sent Lee a check for $25,000 with a letter saying the lesson was the most profitable from a money standpoint that he had ever learned! In five years, this plan was largely responsible for turning the unknown Bethlehem Steel Company into the biggest independent steel producer in the world! And it helped make Charles Schwab a hundred million dollars and the best-known steel man in the world!

"Well," I thought, "if a big man like Charles Schwab, one of the smartest and most practical self-organizers alive, found this simple plan 'the *most profitable* from a money standpoint that he had ever learned,' I'd be a *fool* not to follow it."

Mr. Talbot had told me *what* to do, but he didn't tell me *how!* Now, Charles Schwab showed me *how to do it!*

This "$25,000 Idea" which Charles Schwab said made millions for him gave me that day the vision of a plan which started me on the road to a measure of success that exceeded my wildest dreams!

I am going to show you how I cut my average of closing only
1 sale out of 29 calls, to 1 out of 20; 1 out of 15; 1 out of 10—
and finally 1 out of 3. And how this plan enabled me to increase
the value of my calls from $2.30 to $19 each.

Instead of planning my work from day to day, I hit on the
idea of setting aside every Saturday from 8 A.M. to 1 P.M.—or *all
day*, if necessary. I called it "Self-Organization Day." Each week
I reviewed all my records, brought them up to date and ana-
lyzed them. I laid out my entire week ahead—each day's calls,
Monday through Friday: who I was going to see; when; what I
would say to each person. Between 10:00 and 12:00, I phoned
for appointments. I tried to arrange ten "closing" appointments a week.

I found that you can improve in planning just the same as
you can improve in playing the flute—or anything else that requires practice. Each week I found myself improving. Sometimes, I was able to *partly* set up two and three weeks ahead. All
this required five to six hours of the hardest and most intensive
work I did all week. Within two years, I was able to move Self-
Organization Day up to Friday morning, knock off the rest of
the week, and forget business entirely until Monday morning.

I discovered enormous advantages in planning an entire week
ahead. I telephoned my office each day at 2 P.M., instead of coming in and dawdling at the desk for hours doing things that
didn't amount to very much, or reminiscing with other salesmen until the best part of the day was lost. These were the
things that were keeping me off the street, keeping me from
seeing the people! Whenever I came into the office during the
week, I noticed a difference in my business right away!

I always kept plenty of dimes and nickels in my pocket. Many
of my appointments and business conversations were made from
a pay-station telephone. At times, when it was necessary to come
into the office during the day, I would deliberately walk out, go
around the corner and do my phoning from a pay station to
avoid any trap that might keep me from *seeing the people*.

I was surprised to find that many businessmen preferred to
come into *my* office when I suggested it. Whenever they did, I

cut off all telephone calls and never permitted any other inter-
ruptions. When the interview was terminated, I made it a point
to pick up my hat, go down in the elevator with the client, and
leave him at the front of the building, to get me out of the place.

. . . About that time, I read in Benjamin Franklin's Autobiography: "Early risers, on the average, live to a much older age,
and are more successful." After Ben Franklin found this out,
he began getting up at 5:00 A.M.—so I set my alarm clock an
hour and a half earlier and formed the "Six O'Clock Club."
That gave me an *extra hour* every day for reading and studying
my business; to review my objectives for the day; and give more
thought to what I would say to each person I was going to
call on.

That *quiet hour* in the morning became the *most important
of the day* . . . and I always closed with a prayer I'll tell about
later.

Getting up earlier, I found myself going to bed earlier—but I
thrived on it! When I was going out in the evening, I got home
earlier in the afternoon before dinner, and took a short rest.

I prefer to work on a tight schedule four and a half days a
week and get somewhere, than to be working all the time and
never get anywhere!

I called the plan my "13 Weeks' Self-Organizer." The *machinery* is in the back of this book. This plan of operation literally added ten years to my life! I know this sounds incredible,
but actually it is an understatement. It gave me one of the
greatest luxuries in life, the luxury of having *enough time!*
Time to play; time to rest; time for vacations; time to think
things through; time to study and master to a higher degree
knowledge of my business. Without this plan, it would have
been impossible for me to maintain my enthusiasm . . . and I
*believe if a man can maintain enthusiasm long enough, it will
produce anything!*

Do you want to know how a salesman can increase his sales
in face of increased competition? It's being done by many companies. Let me give you just two examples:

Henry W. Reis, Jr., one of International Business Machines'

sales managers spoke in Boston recently at the 15th New England Sales Management Conference. To the five hundred sales executives in attendance, he said: "I.B.M.'s *Weekly Work Sheet,* the *number one tool* of our salesmen, enabled us to step up the number of calls a salesman is able to make, from 8.8 daily to 10. Results have proved to us once again that there is no substitute for calls in sales work. Salesmen who expose themselves to the most sales opportunities usually get the most signed orders."

Fuller Brush salesmen are breaking their previous all-time records, despite the fact that house to house salesmen are again reporting tougher going. How? "When we noticed a recession in sales," one of their sales managers told me, "we stepped up our calls 5 per cent. It worked for us in 1938, a bad depression year, and now it is working again!"

I firmly believe that comparatively few men fail in selling because they cannot sell. Our failure comes because we lack self-direction and self-discipline.

The great tragedy of the life insurance business is that more than 100,000 salesmen quit every twelve months. *Only one out of ten remains in the business!* I have never been able to find dependable figures to compare this record with other businesses, but I have been told that the overall average is not a whole lot better.

At twenty-nine, in my first year in the business, I was down and out and had quit! Yet twelve years later, at forty-one years of age, I was in a position to retire. Simply by following through from week to week with my "Self-Organizer," I accomplished more in twelve years than I otherwise could have achieved in a lifetime!

3.

A Mathematical Discovery That Raised Me from Ninety-Second to First Place in My Company

BOBBY JONES, one of the greatest golfers of all time, once wrote a book entitled *Down the Fairway*. I found it to be the most interesting and helpful book on golf I ever read. In it he tells about getting into a bad slump one time during a national tournament, and how later he discovered the cause and the cure. Let's listen to *Bobby* himself tell about it:

> . . . and when I got back home to Atlanta, I went out and had a little talk with my old instructor, Stewart Maiden, who to me will always be the first doctor of golf.
>
> Stewart said, "Let's see you hit a few!"
>
> I hit a few. Stewart seemed to be watching my right side. He is a man of few words. "Square yourself around a bit," he said.
>
> I had been playing with a slightly open stance, my right foot and shoulder nearer the line of the shot than the left side.
>
> "Move that right foot and shoulder back a bit," said Stewart.
>
> "Now what do I do?" I asked.
>
> "Knock hell out of it!" said he concisely.
>
> I did. That ball went like a ruled line.

One time I went to *my* "first doctor" of selling: my *records*. Those records showed me my trouble and squared *me* around a bit. And *I* asked "Now what do I do?"

"Knock hell out of it!" my records told me.

I did. The results were unbelievable. Within two years, I was leading all the salesmen of the Fidelity Mutual.

Let me tell you how it happened:

I got to thinking one time: "Why are some men in our company selling three and four times as much insurance as I sell? It's not because they make more calls . . . I don't believe they are four times better salesmen! Yet, I know I am not getting high enough returns on the staggering number of calls I am making."

To get the answer to that, I had to get the facts. Back I went to my records, to study the figures. . . .

I made an astounding discovery!

Right there in black and white, I discovered that 70 per cent of my sales had been closed on the very first interview! Twenty-three per cent of my sales had been closed on the second interview! And *only 7 per cent* of my sales had been closed on the third, fourth, fifth, etc., interviews, which were running me ragged and taking so much of my time.

In other words, I was actually wasting one-half of my working day on a part of my business which was responsible for only 7 per cent of my sales!

But listen to this! Now came the *real* payoff! Some time later, while checking over the names of all the people I sold I found that two-thirds of my sales and my volume had come from *new prospects!* There was the real secret! *New* prospects; *new* leads; *people I had never attempted to sell before!*

It was then simple arithmetic: What was the dollars-and-cents value of each *first* interview? What was the production value of each *new* prospect? What would my production amount to in the next twelve months if I cut out all visits beyond the second interview and concentrate that extra time on *new* prospects?

The answers made my head swim. As I sat there checking and double checking the figures to make sure of my facts, the importance of these discoveries hit me with full force! According to my own records, *I could become the leader of my company!*

I was so excited, I had to get up on my hind legs and walk

around the room. I couldn't have been more emotional if I had already received a telegram from the president of the company congratulating me upon electing myself "President of the Leaders' Club." I could *see* that telegram! I *knew* it would happen. *It was a settled fact with me then and there!*

. . . My figures worked out even better than I hoped for. Within *two years,* this simple mathematical formula raised me from ninety-second to thirteenth, to *first place* in the Fidelity Mutual Life Insurance Company, and I became one of the early million dollar producers in the business.

Now I realize that selling can never be reduced to an exact science any more than medicine can be reduced to an exact science, but it is surprising how many things about selling can be measured and forecast. For example:

One day I was talking with Lawrence J. Doolin, Manager of Agencies for the Fidelity Mutual, the man who conceived the National Quality Award for Life Underwriters, sponsored jointly in the United States and Canada. Larry is one of the keenest sales analysts I have ever known. He said: "Frank, I have noticed when an agent gets those figures $\frac{?}{1}$ upside down—calling on too many old prospects and too few new ones—he is headed for a slump as sure as he lives!"

Then Larry told me about a dinner he attended recently at one of the company's agency meetings. The purpose of the meeting was to arrange for a special anniversary campaign. Enthusiasm was running high!

But can you imagine the expression on the general agent's face, when later in the evening Larry said: "Joe, I don't see how you are going to have a very good month, next month!"

"Why?" asked the astonished general agent.

"Because," predicted Larry, "the reports of your men show a very low ratio of *new* prospects to old!"

"What *did* happen?" I asked Larry.

"They had one of the poorest months in years," he answered.

Lawrence J. Doolin has been summarizing reports and making close analyses of production records from all over the country for more than twenty years. I asked Larry if I might see some combined figures. Let's take a look at them:

Averages over Past Five Years Fidelity Mutual Salesmen	Sales Closed	My Own Averages Published from Speech "Leaders" Convention 30 Years Previously
65%	1st *Selling* Interview	70%
20%	2nd *Selling* Interview	23%
8%	3rd *Selling* Interview	} 7%
7%	4th, 5th, etc., Interview	
100%		100%

Isn't that amazing? These overall figures were compiled from the records over the past five years of new men as well as veteran producers, large and small. It seemed incredible that their figures so closely paralleled my own, originally recorded *more than thirty years before!*

Moreover, Larry Doolin's records of *leading producers* indicate that two-thirds of their sales, interviews, and sales presentations are *consistently* on *new prospects!*

. . . I was discussing these records the other night with Richard W. Campbell of Altoona, Pa., one of the nation's greatest life insurance salesmen, when Dick was visiting with us in our home. As he checked the similarity of these figures with his own, I said: "Dick, how do you account for this?"

Dick was raised on a farm and worked as a farmer before he started selling insurance. He smiled and replied: *"You can't keep threshing the same wheat. You get most of the grain out in the first threshing."*

Now, I don't want to give anyone the impression that I think this same result would work out for you, especially if you are in a different line of selling. But it does prove again the tremendous importance of keeping records, *and analyzing and studying them regularly.*

As I have traveled around the country during the last few years, I've noticed a definite increase in the number of sales managers and executives who make it absolutely *compulsory* for their salesmen to submit records of their activity. Most of them tell me about the great value these records have been to them. Let me give you one example:

For two years a large industrial concern made a study of reports turned in by their entire sales force throughout the nation. They were astonished to find that 80 per cent of all sales were made *after the fifth interview!* But listen to this: They also discovered that 48 per cent of their salesmen made one call on a prospective customer and quit; 25 per cent made two calls and quit; 12 per cent made three and quit; 10 per cent kept calling—*and made 80 per cent of the sales!*

This discovery resulted in such an amazing increase in that company's sales that in their sales training program, staff meetings, and in all their bulletins, they use these figures to emphasize the importance of followup, to make sales.

I have been quite surprised at some managers and salesmen, however, who haven't been so enthusiastic about the value of records. In questioning them closely, I find they kept records all right, *but failed to make much use of the records* . . . somewhat like an aviator who fails to pay attention to his instruments is liable to find himself down over the Azores—without enough gas to get back.

In the next chapter, you will see how I got so far off the course one time that I almost ran out of gas. And how I found my way back on the beam again, before it was too late.

4.

The Biggest Problem of All and How I Licked It

AFTER I STARTED to work on this new formula, two-thirds *new* prospects and one-third old, remember I told you I began to "knock hell out of it"? Well, I did—*for awhile!* Then what happened? You guessed it. *I soon ran out of new prospects!* A setback that looked as though it would kill the whole formula!

So there I was . . . back in the same old rut again.

Then one morning at an agency meeting, Fred Hagen, one of our salesmen who had a million dollar smile and personality, gave a sales demonstration. He was terrific! I was amazed. After the meeting, I asked our manager, Karl Collings, about Fred: "Why isn't Fred Hagen a *big* producer? He seems like even a better salesman than Tom Scott of the Penn Mutual, yet Tom Scott produced ten times as much business last year as Fred did. Why is that?"

"Listen, Frank," Mr. Collings explained, "Fred Hagen *is* a great salesman . . . that is, when he gets in front of a prospect. But he is one of the world's poorest prospectors!"

"What do you mean?" I asked.

"Frank, prospecting is 80 per cent of our sales problem!" declared Collings. "Tom Scott is one of the world's greatest prospectors!"

I had heard a lot about Tom Scott. Reading his record with the Penn Mutual Life Insurance Company sounds like reading Ty Cobb's unapproached record in baseball. Ty led all the batters in the American League twelve out of thirteen years. Tom Scott led all the salesmen in his league for *sixteen* consecutive years! Here was just the man I wanted to talk to about this problem that had me lying awake nights.

I shall be everlastingly grateful to Tom Scott for what he told me.

He said: "Frank, prospecting *is* selling. *Getting leads is just as important as getting applications, because when we stop getting leads, we stop getting applications!*"

"How do you get leads?" I asked him.

"Ask for them!" Tom replied. "Just start asking for them, and you'll teach yourself. Ask everyone you try to sell. I work largely in groups where I have friends and policyholders. I try to get at least two names from everybody I call on."

The talk I had that day with one of the nation's biggest producers shook me awake! I realized then that I either had to lick prospecting—or quit the business!

From that day on, I started to ask everybody I called on for names, regardless of how the interview terminated. I began reading everything I could find on the subject of prospecting. I made it a point to ask every successful producer how *he* did it.

Out of all this, here are the things I did that enabled me to lick this biggest problem of all, and keep myself supplied with more good, substantial leads than I was able to get around to see:

First, I began going back to see every person I had already sold. I soon discovered how stupid I had been to let every sale run into a dead end. I had been walking away from more business than I was selling!

The second man I called on was a mill owner whom I had sold a few weeks previously. He was a typical "old country" German. I said, "Mr. Oppenheimer, you have a son twenty years old. Wouldn't you like to get him started right with some life insurance now, while it costs so little?"

Without a word, he got up from his desk, opened the door leading into the mill: "A-L-F-R-E-D!!" he yelled. His lung power beat any umpire's I had ever heard in baseball. The mill was a city block long and the noise from the machines was deafening. "A-L-F-R-E-D!!" bellowed the big German with greater volume.

At the far end of the mill I saw a handsome young fellow in overalls look around. "COME HERE VUNST!" roared Oppenheimer with a sweeping gesture.

In a few moments, Alfred peeped in. He was built like Jack Dempsey—at that time World Heavyweight Champion. "Did you want to see me, Papa?" he asked meekly.

"The doctor comes tomorrow morning at ten o'clock," gruffly announced Oppenheimer.

"What for, Papa?" asked the boy, surprised.

"Vat for do you think?" asked the old man. "Are you sick?"

"No, I'm not sick."

"All right, we soon find out. The doctor examines you tomorrow morning for insurance!"

"O.K., Papa," said Alfred, giving me a grand smile.

. . . I insured Alfred for $10,000. Not long afterward he was married and began having children of his own, and I sold him substantially more. Later, a younger brother came into the business and I sold him. Finally, I sold everybody in that family.

I don't want to give you the impression that they all worked as quickly as this. They didn't. In fact, it was hard for me at first to ask for names, but as Tom Scott told me, "You teach yourself how, by doing it."

The easiest and most natural place to start, I discovered, was right in the family of a man I had previously sold—his wife, children, brothers, sisters, in-laws, etc. After I had sold two or three in a family circle, my momentum picked up and a lasting friendly relationship developed.

I got a tip one day from my friend J. J. Pocock of Philadelphia, one of the nation's largest distributors of Frigidaire products. He told me that *new* customers were the *best source* of new business. I asked him why. He said: "New customers are enthusiastic and happy about their new purchase. Usually, they are excited and anxious to tell their friends and relations about it. They are proud. You can get more good, red-hot prospects from *new* buyers than from anyone else."

Mr. Pocock backed up his tip with facts from records of his own salesmen and Frigidaire salesmen all over the country. The figures he showed me were so motivating, I found myself out the next day working on this system with more enthusiasm than ever. It worked like magic! It always works. It just can't miss!

I've never forgotten what another top-bracket salesman said to me one time: "Drop me down out of a parachute anywhere in the country and I'll sell! You just get acquainted with one person. He will have relatives, friends, neighbors, business associates and competitors. You soon have customers and the endless chain starts to work. It is *inexhaustible!*"

For many years, I carried a letter around in my pocket. It seldom fails to produce one or more leads whenever I use it. I always have my friend write the letter on *his* letterhead:

> Mr. William R. Jones
> Real Estate Trust Building
> Philadelphia, Pa.
>
> Dear Bill:
>
> I want you to know Frank Bettger. In my opinion, he is one of the best qualified life insurance men in Philadelphia. I have given him my entire confidence, and I have acted on his suggestions.
>
> Maybe you have not been thinking about life insurance, but I know that it will pay you to listen to Mr. Bettger, because he has some very constructive ideas and services which will be of benefit to you and your family.
>
> Sincerely,

It is not always convenient for a man to give me a letter of introduction, so I always carry with me a 4" x 2½" card which reads like this:

TO *Fred W. McBrien*

INTRODUCING

FRANK BETTGER

Ray Kroc

My friend writes the name of the prospect on the upper part of the card, then signs his name at the bottom.

There is a great advantage, I learned, in following up names of prospects *receiving* business from the friend who gives me the lead. However, I am extremely careful to say nothing which might imply that I think I can hold this over them.

I found that such an approach is likely to have a boomerang effect.

I've had many salesmen ask me how I *ask* for leads.

I try to do it in ordinary conversation. A few tactful questions and good listening lead up to it:

"*How did you happen to get started in this business, Mr. McClennen?*"

This question *always* pleases men. The answer frequently runs into quite a bit of time, but I find it very inspirational. I have learned a lot about business and a lot about life in this way. In addition, the story usually brings out names.

Another one of my favorite questions:

"*What do you do when you are not working, Mr. Dixon? In other words, do you have a hobby?*"

By getting a man to talk about himself, his family, friends, business associates, sometimes he tells you about men he plays golf or goes fishing with; sometimes about his competitors, committees he serves on. Then, later in the conversation, I say:

"Mr. Kroll, if your friend Fred McBrien were to walk in here right now, would you hesitate to introduce me to him?"

"Not at all," he usually replies.

Out comes my card of introduction. . . . If I'm talking to someone I've already sold, I say:

"Mr. Ortlip, do you remember how I happened to meet you?"

"Sure," he replies, "my old boss, William Brown, sent you to see me."

"Do you have any regrets that Mr. Brown introduced us?"

"Not at all," is the usual reply.

Out comes my card of introduction.

"You mentioned John Kohler. Would you mind writing his name on the top of this card, and your name at the bottom?"

Usually he says, "No, of course not." Sometimes, he'll give me several others.

If I am stabbing around for a name, I have a favorite expression I like to use:

"Who is the most up-and-coming man you know, under fifty and successful? The kind of man you are!"

Usually, he'll think of two or three who answer this description.

Whenever a man refuses to give me the name of anybody, I say:

"That's all right, Mr. Wright. I think I understand how you feel. I'll tell you what I'll do. Give me the name of someone you know, under fifty, who is making money. I promise you I'll never mention your name."

On that basis, I frequently get some excellent names. When I follow through on a lead like this I always say:

"Mr. Smith, my name is Bettger. I'm in the life insurance business. A mutual friend gave me your name with the understanding that I wouldn't mention his name. He told me that you have been very successful, and that you should be a good man for me to talk to. Could you spare me five minutes now, or would you rather I stop by some other time?"

Usually, he asks me what I want to talk about. I always say, "*You.*"

"If it's about life insurance, I'm not interested," "I'm loaded to the ears"—these replies are nearly always the same. So much so, they often sound rehearsed.

I say: "*That's all right, Mr. Smith, I don't want to talk to you about insurance today. May I have just five minutes?*"

Whether my approach is in person or on the phone, I try never to allow myself to be drawn into a discussion of insurance. My call is for one purpose and for *one purpose alone:* To get five minutes of his time for a fact-finding interview!

Show Appreciation for Leads!

Here is a *must!* Whatever happens when I follow up a lead, good or bad, I always report back promptly to the friend who had the confidence in me to give me the lead. It is a courtesy I have found to be as important as procuring the lead itself. Failure to report back is sure to offend him. He may never mention it, but he may always hold it against you. I know. I have been on both ends; I have felt the unfavorable reaction both as giver and receiver of a recommendation.

Looking back over my career, my biggest regret is that I didn't spend twice as much time calling on, studying, and servicing my clients' interests. I mean that literally and sincerely. I could give a hundred examples right out of my records why it would have paid me much more financially, with less physical effort, and greater happiness.

Repeat sales gradually become more than 50 per cent of our business. I never cease to be surprised by the rapid advances in earning power made by my younger policyholders. Ten years previously, a $5,000 contract looked big to them. Now, $50,000 isn't enough!

So, I found it pays to keep seeing 'em and servicing 'em. They love your interest and sincere enthusiasm for their success. *And they tell you about the newer and bigger connections they've made!*

Mailing Pieces: It's not always possible to see all our clients or customers as often as we would like. Yet, I found, if you stay away too long, and fail to make any contact with them, they become offended and *forget you!*

So, in addition to birthday cards and age change reminders, one of the best investments I ever made was to send out a monthly mailing piece. There are some very fine services of this kind to which you can subscribe. A good mailing piece maintains a continuous contact, builds prestige, and reminds your friend that you are thinking of him.

Playing Position for the Next Shot!

A discouraged young man came to me about a year ago for advice. He had been trying to sell life insurance for fourteen months. In the beginning he did pretty well, he said, but after he had sold a few friends and college fraternity brothers, he didn't know how to go on. Now, he was so disheartened he was about ready to give up.

I questioned him for awhile and found that every sale he made he allowed to run into a dead end. Here's what I said to him:

"John, you've only done *half* the job. Go back and get at least two leads from every man you have sold. Remember, *after* you have sold a man, nothing gives him more assurance than he has made a really wise decision, than *when you ask him for names!*

"When you ask a man for a lead, do you know what you are doing? In a sense, you're asking him to write out an *additional* check for $21—payable to you, personally. If you get three leads, he's drawing a check to your order for $63! That's not a theory, it's a *fact!—based on your own records!* That's not bad, is it?

"In addition, John, ask everybody you call on for names, regardless of how your interview terminates. *Some of the best sales I ever made have been to men whose names I got from people I never sold!*"

At the end of our talk, the young man thanked me earnestly and said: "This has taught me a lesson I've always needed."

Six months later, he came into my office. I never saw a more excited and enthusiastic salesman. He said, "Mr. Bettger, I made it a point to try to get at least two names from everybody I called on, regardless of how the interview terminated."

I was almost as excited as he was. I said, "What happened?"

"I've got over five hundred good names, more than I can get around to see."

"What about your production?" I asked.

"I've paid for $238,000 the first six months of this year. With the cases I've got in the mill," he said, "I'll go *over a half million* this year!"

...And he did!

SUMMARY
AND MAGIC PHRASES

PART ONE

1. *A $25,000 Idea!* If you want to add ten years to your life; if you want to enjoy one of the greatest luxuries in life, the luxury of having enough time —time to play; time to rest; time to think things through; time to get things done; and know that you have done them to the best of your ability:

   Set aside one morning each week—*all day,* if necessary. Call it "Self-Organization Day."

   The whole secret of freedom from anxiety over not having enough time lies not in working more hours, but in the proper planning of hours!

2. Selling can never be reduced to an exact science any more than medicine can be reduced to an exact science, but it is amazing how many things about selling can be measured and forecast. Successful sales executives have found they can be of the greatest help to their salesmen by making it absolutely compulsory for them to keep records and *analyze them regularly!* So, if you want to avoid slumps and keep your sales at a high level, keep records and analyze them at the end of each week. It is your *Insurance for Success in Selling!*

3. *The Biggest Problem of All and How to Lick It:* Remember the sage advice of Tom Scott:

Prospecting *is* selling. Getting leads is just as important as getting applications, because when we stop getting leads, we stop getting applications!

Never let a sale run into a dead end. Always "play position for the next shot."

Magic Phrases That Produce Names and Leads:

How did you happen to get started in this business, Mr. McClennen?

What do you do when you are not working, Mr. Dixon? In other words, do you have a hobby?

Mr. Kroll, if your friend Fred McBrien were to walk in here right now, would you hesitate to introduce me to him?

Mr. Ortlip, do you remember how I happened to meet you? (He answers affirmatively.) . . . *Do you have any regrets that Mr. Brown introduced me?* ("Not at all" is the usual reply.) . . . *You mentioned John Kohler. Would you mind writing his name on the top of this card, and your name at the bottom?*

Who is the most up-and-coming man you know, under fifty and successful? The kind of man you are! (If a man refuses to give the name: *That's all right, Mr. Wright. I think I understand how you feel. I'll tell you what I'll do. Give me the name of someone you know, under fifty, who is making money. I promise you I'll never mention your name.*)

4. *Show Appreciation for Leads.* Here is a *must!* Whatever happens when you follow up a lead, good

or bad, always report back promptly to the friend who had the confidence in you to give you the lead. It is a courtesy as important as procuring the lead itself. Failure to report back is sure to offend him. He may never mention it, but he may always hold it against you.

Never forget a customer; never let a customer forget you.

If finding prospects is not one of your problems, finding *interested* prospects no doubt is. Apply these same methods for the next thirteen weeks, and you may find that *you* have been walking away from more business than you have sold.

Little Things That Made Me A Better Salesman—No. 1

HOW I LEARNED TO LICK THE DEPRESSION

Just as I was leaving the office one day, Al Gould, for years one of the company's leading producers, stopped me and asked: "How are you doing, Frank?"

"Pretty well, Mr. Gould," I answered. "How are you doing?"

"Well," he said, "it looks like a bad year to me. This *depression*—I don't know how long it's going to keep up—but it looks as though it's bound to last through the whole year anyhow."

"What do you mean, depression?" I asked, surprised.

"Why," he said, "don't you know there's a depression on?"

"No," I replied. "I don't know anything about a depression."

"Where have you been?" asked Al. "Don't you ever read anything? *We're in the middle of a depression!*"

"No," I had to admit, "I didn't know anything about it."

Well then Al started. He had made a study of the whole situation and explained to me about the economic conditions and so forth that brought this depression on. The more he talked, the more I realized how stupid and dumb I was and that I hadn't any right to be out selling insurance as I'd been. When I left there that day, I knew it was impossible to sell life insurance as long as that depression kept up.

The next week what do you think happened? You're right. *Nothing!* I stopped making calls as though I was afraid of being hit with a bomb on the way there. At the end of three weeks, my production hadn't just dropped down. It had dropped out! Totally and completely.

Then one day I got to thinking: "Here now, this is *silly!* Before Mr. Gould told me about the depression, I was doing all right. Now that I understand it, I have quit selling, and the only reason I know of is that I have *quit making the calls.*"

All the rest of that day I spent *preparing,* the way I did before I found out anything was wrong, preparing an entire week's work in advance.

In a short time, I was right back into production. And at the end of the year, I had led the entire Fidelity Mutual field force throughout the country!

But Al Gould had one of the worst years he ever had in his life.

At our agency's first meeting in January, the following year, Mr. Gould was the speaker. His subject was "Outlook for the New Year." Summed up, I thought the talk should have been called *"Look Out for the New Year!"* As he finished, Austin Gough, one of our energetic young salesmen, sprang to his feet and said: "Mr. Chairman, may I make a motion?"

"Sure, go ahead," said the Chairman.

"I would like to move that the younger men of this agency challenge the older men to a sixty-day contest!"

Everybody laughed. It really was funny. The older men outnumbered the younger men and, based on past performance, it was like a Class D league team challenging the World's Champions. But in a spirit of fun, the older fellows accepted the challenge.

After the meeting, I called the young men together and said: "Let's have a little meeting of our own, a secret conference." So we got together and I told them the story about Al Gould's explaining to me several months before about the depression, the effect it had on me, and then what happened later. They had a big laugh and all agreed to *forget* the depression—to stop reading and listening to all this depression talk, and really get out and *make the calls!*

At the end of sixty days, we had actually beaten the older men two to one. At the Monday morning meeting following the contest, I told the "Al Gould Story" to the entire agency, just as I had told it to the younger men. Everybody laughed at the "Big Bad Wolf!"

... From then on, as I have called on businessmen, if any of them try to talk "hard times and depression" I tell them the Al Gould Depression Story, and we always have a good chuckle. *Then, I've got a chance to do business with them!*

PART TWO

My Entire Selling Process—
Step by Step

5.

The Most Difficult Step in the Sale and How I Handle It

WHICH DO YOU think is the most difficult step in the sale?

I have asked this question of thousands of sales people all over the country. Many of them say, "The close." But the great majority of leading salesmen have told me, "It is not the close at all; it is the *approach!*"

When I first learned this, I began to understand why I got so nervous and frequently paced up and down outside a man's office before going in to see him. I didn't know *how* to approach him! I was afraid of being turned down without having an opportunity to tell my story.

Many sales people believe that the first ten words are the most important.

One great national sales organization developed a superb model for an approach. It has been used successfully thousands of times by their salesmen throughout the country. It helped me. And it will help *anyone* who uses it as a pattern:

After introducing himself, the salesman says: *"Mr. Gray, I would like to show you our modern cash register. It will do three things for you: prevent losses in your store; increase your profits; and increase your business."*

It is brief; it appeals to the other person's point of view; and it gives three vitally important things your product will do for *him!*

In May, 1945, while conducting a sales clinic in Enid, Oklahoma, I was told about a retail shoe salesman named Dean

Niemeyer who was attending our clinic. Dean had just established what may have been a world record by selling 105 pairs of shoes in one day! Each sale was a separate, individual sale, made to eighty-seven women and children. Here was a man I wanted to talk to. I wanted to see him in *action!* So I went around to the store where Mr. Niemeyer worked and asked him how he did it. He said: "It is all in the approach. A customer is either sold or missed by the way she is approached at the front door."

I was anxious to see just what he meant, so I watched him in action part of that morning. He really makes the customer feel at home. He goes out and meets her at the door with a sincere, warmhearted smile. If it's an old customer, he says: *"Good morning, Mrs. Young. Let me help you!"*

If he doesn't know her, he says: *"Good morning. My name is Niemeyer, what's yours?"* (This always pleases the new customer; she returns his smile and is glad to tell *her* name.) With Dean's natural, easy, helpful manner, the customer feels glad she came into the store. *She is sold before she sits down.*

After the sale, when Dean hands the customer her wrapped purchases, he says: *"Thank you, Mrs. Young. Come back soon again, will you?"* With his enthusiastic smile, you just *know* he appreciated her business. Every customer returns his smile and to his question *"Come back soon again, will you?"* she replies "I will" as though she means it. And Dean's record proves that she means it.

As I walked down the street, I gave Dean Niemeyer *100 per cent.* And *I* was mighty glad *I* had gone into that store. In fact, I have been giving this little talk to retail sales people ever since. And I have had wonderful reports of the results from all over the country.

I can enthusiastically recommend every sales person to use it until it becomes just as natural to him as breathing.

Here is the "approach talk" I use, which became invaluable to me in making men willing to listen and answer my questions. In fact, it proved to be literally a gold mine! I gave a variation of it in my book, *From Failure to Success in Selling,* but I have always regretted that I failed to analyze it in that book. So now, I'll give the talk, composed of only four sentences, then I will analyze each sentence and try to explain the psychology back of it. I like to think of it as "The Sale Before the Sale."

After the man knows who I am, and my business, here is what I say . . . the *exact* words:

ME. Mr. Edwards, I can't tell by the color of your eyes or the color of your hair what your situation is, any more than if I walked in to the best dentist in Philadelphia, sat down in his chair and refused to open my mouth—he couldn't do very much for me, could he? (*Always with a big grin.*)

EDWARDS. No. (*Ninety-nine times out of one hundred he smiles and says "No."*)

ME. Well, that's my position with you, unless you are willing to take me into your confidence to a certain degree. In other words, in order that I may show you something at a future date that might be of value to you, would you mind if I ask you a few questions?

EDWARDS. Go ahead. What are the questions?

ME. Now, Mr. Edwards, if I ask you some questions you do not care to answer, you won't offend me. I'll understand. But if anybody ever knows anything about what you tell me, it will be because *you* tell them, not because *I* do. It is in strict confidence. Right?

EDWARDS. Right!

Let's analyze it:

First Sentence:

What could be more ridiculous than to walk into a dentist's office, sit down in his chair, then refuse to open your mouth? . . . So when I say "He couldn't do very much for me, could he?" the prospect *always* smiles and replies, "No."

Second Sentence:

"Well, that's my position with you, unless you are willing to take me into your confidence *to a certain degree*." . . . I used to say: "Unless you are willing to take me into your confidence." . . . Well, I found that was asking *too much* in the first minute. One day, as I said this to a man and I saw him tighten up, I happened to add four words, *"to a certain degree."* He immediately relaxed and it seemed to disarm him completely.

Third Sentence:

"In other words, in order that I may show you something at a future date that might be of value to you, would you mind if I ask you a few questions?"

I find they love that *"future date"!* It tells a man you are not there to put on pressure and try to sell him anything today. So, he can relax and answer your questions freely and truthfully, without fear that you are going to use his answers against him today. It's surprising the difference that makes!

". . . might be of value to you." There is nothing in these words to imply that, even at a future date, you are coming back to *sell* him. When I say this, I think he senses that I mean it *sincerely.* At this point I really am *not* thinking of a *sale.* I am thinking *precisely what I say.*

"Would you mind if I ask you a few questions?" For a while, I used *"some"* questions. Later, I found it better to say a *"few"* questions.

By now, he is not only willing, but seems anxious for me to go ahead with the questions. So, starting from scratch, in less than one minute, this man is willing to take me into his confidence. However, I am going to ask him some very intimate, private questions. So experience taught me to go just one step farther. . . .

Fourth Sentence:

"Now, Mr. Edwards, if I ask you some questions you do not care to answer, you won't offend me. I'll understand. But if anybody ever knows anything about what you tell me, it will be because you tell them, not because I do. It is in strict confidence. Right?" . . . As I say *"Right?"* I nod my head, and he usually returns the nod, and repeats, *"Right!"*

I have found this fourth sentence *magic!* I have used it

thousands of times. It is the punch line in my *"sale before the sale."*

I am largely indebted to my good friend, Richard W. Campbell of Altoona, Pa., for the perfection of this confidence-gaining approach talk. Dick has used it with amazing success for many years.

After I began developing the two-interview system, I gradually got away from attempting to do very much selling on the first call. However, I don't want to give anyone the impression that I discontinued selling on the first interview *entirely*. All through the book you will see situations where the "green light" was flashed in the first interview—sometimes right in the first thirty seconds! Some of my most exciting sales have been closed in the very first contact.

I realize that many salesmen operate entirely on a standardized approach designed to sell on the first interview. I would not urge anyone to give up this method if he is successful. After you have made your initial sale and later get around to analyzing your customer's complete needs, you will find this one-minute, fact-finding approach talk amazingly effective. You may not use the exact words—but *don't* lengthen the talk.

Many companies now provide their salesmen with organized presentations and sales talks. If they are prepared by men who have had successful sales experience, that's good. I have seen some excellent ones. However, never, *never* memorize these talks or *any* talk word for word. It's a *rare* person who can deliver a memorized talk naturally, and nobody wants to listen to a canned speech or canned sales talk.

I found the advice of an old time "stock actor" sound. He said, "Frank, never memorize anything. Read whatever you want to remember several times each day at short intervals. Then suddenly, one day you *know* it. If you learn it that way, it will never sound 'canned.' Give your talk to your wife, your manager, or another salesman. Rehearse it over and over until you know it so well it becomes as natural as breathing."

6.

How I Get All the Facts and Prepare for the Selling Interview

I'VE HAD SOME ABLE salesmen tell me they can't use a questionnaire; that as soon as they pull it out, the prospect freezes right up on them.

I had the same experience myself, until I hit on a very simple technique which quickly overcame this difficulty. Here it is:

I never pull the questionnaire out at first. I find that I get into my questions much more smoothly if I begin by asking one or two of the questions *before* I do that. While the prospect is talking, I am looking straight into his face with absorbed interest—then out comes the paper in a *routine manner*—never taking my eyes away from his eyes.

I am not sneaking it out. Yet, I'm sure he isn't conscious of my removing anything from my pocket. In fact, I am hardly conscious of it myself, because I am listening so intently to what he is saying.

Still watching him, I unfold the paper; deliberately lay it down without ever looking at it.

From *then* on, I go right through the questions as rapidly as possible, much the same as the doctor does in making his examination. It takes me from five to ten minutes, depending upon how much *he* talks.

I put the paper back in my pocket in the same manner that I take it out. My last question does it. (With a smile) "Mr. Edwards, what do you do when you're not working? In other words, do you have a hobby?"

His answer to this question frequently becomes valuable to me at a later date.

While he is answering that question, I return the questionnaire to my pocket.

I never show it to him or discuss it with him in the first interview. His curiosity in the meantime will develop to such an extent that it helps me immensely in the second interview.

If his answer to my question about his hobby is too short, I ask another question that I eventually ask every person I ever meet:

"Mr. Edwards, how did you happen to get started in this business?"

There seems to be something magic in this question. It has frequently helped me get a favorable interview and a questionnaire completed on men who never before opened up with anyone else.

Frequently, there has been a time limit agreed on for the first interview, so when my five or ten minutes are up, I say: "Well, my five minutes are up. Is there anything else you would like to tell me, Mr. Edwards?"

As soon as he answers that question, I stand up and shake hands with him to show my appreciation for his confidence, and say: "Thank you for your confidence, Mr. Edwards. I would like to do some thinking about the information you've given me. I've got an idea that may be of some value to you, and after I work it out, I'll give you a call for an appointment. Is that satisfactory?"

Rarely does he object.

I use my judgment at that moment to decide whether to arrange a definite appointment for a later date, say for the following week.

Now then, let's have a look at the questionnaire, and Mr. Edwards' answers. I didn't make it up as a sample. I pulled a few out of my files and use this one for illustration. The only change is in the man's name:

File No. _____

PERSONAL ESTATE INVENTORY

(CONFIDENTIAL INFORMATION)

1. Assured Income I will need:
    (1) Wife Minimum Mo. Income $_____
    (2) Yourself at age 65 $_____
    (3) Other purposes _____ $_____
                Total $_____
    On the basis of a net return of 10% to produce the
    above assured annual income will require a princi-
    pal sum of $_____

2. Additional Capital I will need:
    (1) For Education:
            (Expenses of education of children, immedi-
            ate convenience of widow and other family
            needs.) Mother: $_____ $_____
    (2) For liquidation of Specific Obligations:
            (Such as mortgages, accrued income tax, Fed-
            eral Estate and State Inheritance Taxes, Ad-
            ministration Expenses.) $_____
    (3) For Business Purposes:
            (To effect settlements, purchase stock, insur-
            ance on lives of valuable executives.) $_____
    (4) Notes: { Personal $_____
                        { As Endorser $_____
    (5) For Funeral Expenses:
            (Doctor's Fees, Costs of Illness, Current Bills,
            etc.) $_____
    (6) Immediate Cash, 3 x Monthly Income $_____

           TOTAL CAPITAL I NEED $_____

3. Value of my Present Estate:

    (1) Insurance now in force $_____

Company	Amount	Kind	Premium
Penn	5000	20 Pay	
"	5000	O.L.	
Prudential	1000	20 Pay	Payable to Mother

    (2) Securities, Stocks, Bonds, etc, $_____

    (3) Business Interests $_____

    (4) Real Estate $_____

    (5) Cash on Hand $_____

    (6) Earned Income from Other Sources _____

    (7) Gross Annual Income: $_____   _____

    (8) Inheritance   NONE

         TOTAL $_____

4. Additional Capital I still need to meet
    my requirements: .... $_____

Name: Arthur C. Edwards ....Birth Date: 6–2–38

Wife: Alice E. Edwards ......Birth Date: 7–10–44

Wife's Income: None ....

Sons: Arthur C., Jr. 9-20-74 ...Daughters: Anna Mae 2-15-72

....

....

Do you have a Will? No.......Date Drawn?................

Wife's Will: No.............Date Drawn?................

Appointment: Phone....................................

FRANK BETTGER
1420 Western Saving Fund Building, Philadelphia 7, Pa.
Confidential File

My *questionnaire*—actually a Personal Estate Inventory and "Balance Sheet" of a man's financial life—is based on *one* principle—the soundest and most important secret of success in selling anything:

Finding out what people want, and helping them get it.

I like to think of it as *his* "Balance Sheet."

And remember: the "additional capital I still need to meet my requirements" is *set by him—the prospect himself!*

Let me repeat: I do not show the "Balance Sheet" to the prospect in the first interview. I never make any figures in his presence. I do the figuring and preparing of his case in my own office on Friday morning, "Self-Organization Day." My objective is to obtain two questionnaires daily, four days a week for forty-five weeks. This assures me over three hundred good closing interviews a year. Three hundred good *closing* interviews will produce from fifty to one hundred sales for any salesman. Let me give you an example:

I once read about the famous New York criminal lawyer, Samuel S. Leibowitz, who had the reputation of winning extremely difficult cases with what seemed to be great ease. He was asked one time, after he'd won a most remarkable case: *"At what point in the trial did you win this case?"*

"I won the case a month before the trial opened," he replied. "When I went into the courtroom, I had the answers to every bit of evidence the District Attorney could use against me. This involved a great deal of work."

In an interview later, Leibowitz said: "In preparing for a trial, I make up a list of things which are against my client and then list all the things in his favor. The opposing attorney cannot surprise me with evidence to which I have no answer!"

This was the secret of Samuel Leibowitz's great success. And I've found this to be the secret of the success of every outstanding salesman and businessman I have ever come to know.

In a small way, I try to follow the same principle. On Friday morning, after completing the "Balance Sheet," I prepare an analysis showing my observations and recommendations. Then I feel confident that I have the answers to every objection that might be raised. When I close a sale, I feel just as that famous lawyer said: *"I* won the case a week *before* the trial opened."

. . . All right. Now my case is prepared. I am ready to phone for an appointment. I say: "I have something to show you that I believe might be of value to you. Would it be convenient for you to see me one day next week?"

Now we come to the *selling* interview!

7.

The Selling Interview

THIS INTERVIEW with Mr. Edwards took place in the evening at his home. (First, let me say this: I keep everything simple. Even if a man's estate is large, my proposal does not produce the thorough analysis that a lawyer or trust company will make at a later date—but it does accomplish what I regard as the chief objective of the salesman, which in this case is *to provide the cash needed!*)

When I arrived, I was introduced to his wife and two small children. I visited with the children until Mrs. Edwards took them off to bed. When she came downstairs, she and her husband waited for me to talk, but I waited for them. I always let my prospects talk about anything they want to talk about. I'm not particular; just as long as they talk. . . .

Soon, Mr. Edwards asked: "Did you have something you wanted to show us?" I showed them the "Balance Sheet" and asked Mrs. Edwards to explain it to me. She did it surprisingly well. She discussed various items freely. When they got down to: "Additional Capital I Will Need to Meet My Requirements —over $100,000," they were shocked. Prospects always are. The figure is always considerably in excess of the amount of insurance they can or are willing to buy immediately. But I never cease to be surprised how quickly it adjusts their thinking and raises their sights.

Then I handed to Mr. and Mrs. Edwards each an original copy of their Personal Estate Analysis. . . .

(The wife is always pleased to see her name on the face of the paper jointly with her husband's. If the interview takes place

48

at the husband's office, I find he generally takes it home. When his wife sees her name as *equal partner,* she is likely to be on my team.)

I suggested that they read it through quietly, and we could discuss it afterward. . . .

(I always have a yellow, unbound carbon copy with me, and time my reading with my prospects'. I never open my mouth while they read. That silence is golden! *Some sort of magic is going on there.*)

PERSONAL

ESTATE ANALYSIS

for

ARTHUR C. EDWARDS

and

ALICE E. EDWARDS

YOUR FAMILY RECORD

	Date of Birth
Arthur C. Edwards	June 2, 1938
Alice E. Edwards	July 10, 1944
Anna Mae Edwards	Feb. 15, 1972
Arthur C. Edwards, Jr.	Sept. 20, 1974

YOUR LIFE INSURANCE ESTATE

Company	Amount	Kind	Age	Date of Issue	Bene-ficiary	How Payable	Cash Value at Age 65
Prudential	$_____	20 Pay Life	31	8/18/31	MOTHER	Lump Sum	$_____
Penn Mutual	$_____	20 Pay Life	35	11/18/42	ALICE	Lump Sum	$_____
Penn Mutual	$_____	Ordinary Life	40	1948	ALICE	Lump Sum	$_____
	$_____						$_____

GENERAL ESTATE

Business Interest . . . . $_____
Real Estate . . . . $_____
Cash on Hand . . . . $_____
Total . . . . $_____

OBJECTIVES

SET BY YOU

1. A fund to cover your last illness, funeral expenses and related expenses $_____

2. A lump sum for your mother $_____

3. Liquidation of Mortgage, Accrued Income Tax, Current Bills, etc. $_____

                 Total $_____

4. An absolutely dependable income, guaranteeing for ALICE a sufficient amount during your children's dependency years $_____

5. An absolutely dependable income, guaranteed for ALICE'S life, through her declining years $_____

6. To save and build for yourself a certain backlog income, sufficient to make you independent and comfortable in your old age $_____

RECOMMENDATIONS

A. That you execute a simple will, giving all
   your property to ALICE, if living, otherwise to your children.

   Note: Your attorney will draw up such
   a Will for a small fee.

B. That ALICE execute a similar Will.

1. We urge you to continue carrying your present policies, just as they are, to provide the
   necessary cash for expenses incident to
   death; Lump Sum for your Mother; liquidation of mortgage; accrued income tax,
   current bills, etc. and one year readjustment
   period following your death. $_____

2. In order to accomplish your minimum objectives during your children's dependency
   years, we would suggest that you immediately purchase $_____ of additional life
   insurance on the Ordinary Life Plan, with
   Family Maintenance rider. This would provide ALICE and your Children with an income of $_____ month for 20 years from
   the date of your death—then a life income
   thereafter for ALICE, as shown on the next
   page. $_____ *

* This income would be increased by Social Security benefits, until each child
  reaches Age 18.

3. The Family Maintenance rider included in the above contract is made up of term insurance, which you may convert gradually as you are able to invest more money, to provide a retirement income for yourself at Age 60 or 65. You may convert this rider during the first ten years, without a medical re-examination.

SUMMARY

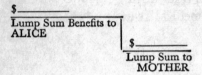

PRESENT PLAN

$_____
Lump Sum Benefits to
ALICE

$_____
Lump Sum to
MOTHER

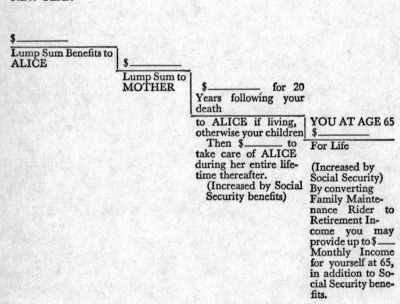

NEW PLAN

$_____
Lump Sum Benefits to
ALICE

$_____
Lump Sum to
MOTHER

$_____ for 20 Years following your death

to ALICE if living, otherwise your children Then $_____ to take care of ALICE during her entire lifetime thereafter.
(Increased by Social Security benefits)

YOU AT AGE 65
$_____
For Life

(Increased by Social Security) By converting Family Maintenance Rider to Retirement Income you may provide up to $____ Monthly Income for yourself at 65, in addition to Social Security benefits.

After they finished reading, I looked at Mr. Edwards and asked my usual question: *"How do you like it?"*

"I think I like it," he replied.

THERE WAS A BUYING SIGNAL!

I said, *"Good.* I would like my friend, Dr. Towson, to check you over and see whether you are as good on the inside as you look on the outside. If he says you are all right, then I want to bring the contract myself, so that you may see how perfectly it carries out your wishes. Will you be in your office tomorrow morning about 11:15?"

"I would rather not be examined yet," said Mr. Edwards, "I want to think it over for awhile."

"Would there be any harm in our company thinking you over while you are thinking us over?" I asked.

"I suppose not," he agreed.

"Fine," I said, then I began asking him questions and filling out the application form.

I always mark a heavy X where the buyer signs. I handed him my pen, pointing to the X and said: "Will you write your name here, the same as I have filled it in at the top?"

He signed without a word.

Then I said: "Do you want to give me your check for the full year, Mr. Edwards, or would you rather just pay half now, and the balance in six months?"

He discussed it with his wife, and they finally decided to pay on a quarterly basis the first year.

So, with just a little persuasion, Mr. Edwards bought the plan exactly as it was drawn up. Most people, however, like to procrastinate, and our big job is to sell the *now!* In the next two chapters particularly, and all through the book, you will see methods I have found effective in making people *want* to buy, and *do it now!*

MAGIC PHRASES

How Do You Like It?

It is surprising how frequently the prospect answers: "I think I like it." *There is a* BUYING SIGNAL! I assume this means he is going to buy, so I don't wait another moment. I say, *"Good"* and I begin to close. I ask the necessary questions and write his answers on the application (order form), starting with some easy questions: "Let's see, Mr. Edwards, your office address is Medical Arts Building, isn't it?" Once they begin answering the questions, they seldom balk.

When I try to arrange an appointment for the medical examination, if he says: "I want to think it over for awhile," I say:

Would there be any harm in our company thinking you over, while you are thinking us over?

8.

An Invaluable Lesson on Closing I Learned from an "Old-Timer"

IN THE BEGINNING of the book, I told how my records showed that, over a period of years, I was gradually able to cut down my average of closing only one sale out of twenty-nine calls, to one out of three. The real beginning of this improvement I owe to an old-timer, Billy Walker of Atlantic City.

I seemed to do pretty well, until it came time for action, then the interview usually terminated about like this: "Well, Mr. Bettger, I'll think it over. See me sometime after the first of the month, and I'll let you know what I'm going to do."

The staggering amount of time spent in following up *old* prospects again and again, with no results, was tragic. I began to despise my work.

In discussing this problem with older and more experienced salesmen, I heard that William C. Walker, then manager of our company's Atlantic City office, was noted for being a great "closer." Billy had built a successful and enthusiastic agency, covering the southern half of the state of New Jersey. He went out with each of his men and showed them how he closed sales on the *first selling interview!*

Here was just the man I wanted to talk to.

So one day, I called Mr. Walker on the long distance phone and asked if I might see him if I came down to Atlantic City. He asked me "What about?" I frankly told him. He said, "Come down and sit in on our agency meeting on Saturday morning."

That morning, Mr. Walker gave a sales demonstration of an actual sale he had closed that week. One of his salesman took the part of the buyer. Billy really was a great closer! I wondered how anybody ever got away from him!

After the meeting, he took me into his private office and I told him about my trouble. To my surprise, he said: "I know just what you mean. I went all through that *myself!* People, in large cities especially, think it's so easy for a salesman to call back again and again, they'll try to stall you off every time."

"How do you overcome this?" I asked.

"When I began traveling over a large territory," smiled Billy, "I soon realized it was impossible for me to be running back, so I just began holding on longer. When you've *got* to do it, you *can* do it! *It's all in your state of mind!*"

"What do you do, Mr. Walker, when a man says, 'I'm not interested,' or, 'I'm not in the market just now,' or, 'I couldn't possibly afford it now,' etc."

> *"You never know what's in a man's mind by what he says,"* declared Billy. *"When a man offers objections, he doesn't mean he won't buy. What he* REALLY *means is that you haven't convinced him yet. You haven't produced enough evidence to make him* WANT *to buy!"*

The following week, I began imagining I was working under Billy Walker and would have to make my report to him at his Saturday morning meeting, as his other men did. *"I must win or lose on the first selling interview!"*

It made a great difference immediately! I soon discovered the significance of what Billy Walker had said to me:

"YOU NEVER KNOW WHAT'S IN A MAN'S MIND BY WHAT HE SAYS."

I don't want to give anyone the impression that I am a high-pressure salesman. That is if I understand what the term "high pressure" means. Just so long as I can forget myself and what I am going to make out of a sale, and keep my mind on the other person and what *he* will get out of the sale, I have no fear of creating the impression that I am high pressure.

9.

How Questions Converted a Skeptic into an Enthusiastic Buyer

M Y COMPANY gave me a lead one day on a man named John Bowers. (The name is fictitious, but in every other respect the details of this unusual case are true.) Mr. Bowers was a manufacturers' agent, recently transferred from New York City. About a year before moving to Philadelphia, he had bought a small "educational policy" for his son.

In my first interview, I quickly found he was the "silent type." My usual approach talk failed to get me anywhere. He soon cut me off with: *"I don't believe in life insurance!"*

You could tell he *really* meant it!

Standing on his desk, directly in front of him, was a large framed picture of his wife and boy. I said, "That's a lovely picture. Is that your wife and boy?"

He nodded yes, and said: "We've got a new baby daughter, too."

"Congratulations!" I said, shaking his hand with enthusiasm. "How old is your new baby?"

"Three months," he replied.

I asked what her name was and found they had named her after his wife, Katharine.

"That's *perfect*. Let me see," I said thoughtfully, "that brings up another situation, doesn't it?"

"What's that?" he asked, getting a little friendly.

"You've got an endowment policy for John's education. You'll want one for Katharine, won't you?" I suggested.

"Sure," he agreed without hesitation, as though he were glad I brought it up. "Do you want to fix that up for me?"

"You bet your life!" I smiled and said. Out came my pink juvenile application form, and I began asking the questions. He signed without a word.

Then, I said, "Mr. Bowers, you are going to make these payments each year yourself, aren't you?"

"Certainly," he replied.

"For only a small extra amount, we put a clause in your contract, waiving all future payments if you should die. In other words, if anything should happen to you, Mrs. Bowers would have no more payments to worry about," I explained.

He wanted to know what a "small" extra payment amounted to. When he found it was only a few dollars, he told me to put the clause in both John's and Katharine's policies.

I laid a white application form on the desk in front of him: *"Right here,"* I said in a routine manner, pointing to the X. He signed without any questions.

"How long has it been since you have had a physical examination, Mr. Bowers?" I asked.

"Not since I was in the Navy. Do I have to be examined for this?" He looked annoyed.

"Oh, sure," I smiled, "but you won't have any trouble. If you are as good on the inside as you look on the outside, you'll have these policies back in a few days. You are feeling well this morning, aren't you?"

"Sure, I'm not afraid of any examination they want to give me," he assured me.

"Good," I smiled. "Will it be all right if I have our doctor come over tomorrow morning, say about 10:15?"

We agreed on a time, and I left without attempting to get any more information from him. He had told me, with so much bitterness in his voice, that "he didn't believe in life insurance," I didn't want to risk a setback at this point. I knew he never suspected what this examination might lead him to in a short time.

A few days later, I delivered those two "Educational" contracts to him. They were only $1,000 policies, and he gave me a check for the annual premiums. Then I said, "Mr. Bowers, I want to congratulate you on the splendid examination you passed. On the strength of that examination, I could get you $50,000 of life insurance."

"Well, I'm glad I passed, all right," said he, looking pleased, "but I don't want any insurance for myself. You know I told you that I don't believe in life insurance."

"That's entirely all right. You are the sole judge of that," I assured him.

Now was the time for me to get my questionnaire completed! Here's what happened:

ME. Mr. Bowers, I can't tell by the color of your eyes, or the color of your hair what your situation is. . . .

(And *this time,* he let me go right through with my "approach" talk!) When I came to the time for asking questions, he said:

"Go ahead."

I went through the questions very rapidly. To my surprise, he answered everything without hesitation. In fact, when I came to such questions as real estate, mortgages, cash on hand, earned income, he answered them *proudly.* I was amazed at the amounts he stated. My last question: "What do you do when you are not working . . . in other words, do you have a hobby?" gave me another surprise. He had a boat that he spent a lot of time on during the summer, fishing, etc. The boat cost him $7,500!

He talked quite awhile about the boat and his fishing. When he was finished, I said, "Thank you for your confidence, Mr. Bowers, and let me repeat, if anybody knows anything about what you tell me, it will be because you tell them, not because *I* do. It is in strict confidence. Right?"

"Just so you don't try to sell me any insurance," he warned.

About a week later, I called him on the phone and asked if I might see him Monday morning.

"What about?" he asked coldly.

"I've got some information I want to show you," was my answer.

"What about?" he repeated.

"You! Something I think you ought to see!"

He agreed to see me, but said I'd better make it about two o'clock in the afternoon.

When I arrived, there was a note on his office door. "Leave deliveries in garage. I am at 1518 Pine Street."

I didn't know what to do. "Well," I thought, "he made an appointment with me, and he left this address (his home address). So I'll take a chance . . . it's not far from here."

His wife came to the door when I rang. I told her I had an appointment with Mr. Bowers. She left me standing on the step outside, but came back in a few moments and invited me in.

Mr. Bowers was resting on a sofa in the living room. He didn't look too pleased to see me, but he introduced me to Mrs. Bowers as "the man who took care of John's and the baby's Educational Policies." She smiled politely but immediately left the room. I could hear both children as she closed the door behind her.

He told me to sit down then said, yawning: "What was it you wanted to show me?"

I opened my briefcase, handed him the *Estate Analysis.* I held onto the carbon copy and said: "Now, Mr. Bowers, if you don't mind, I am just going to sit here quietly while you read."

(Let me emphasize and *re-emphasize* that at this point of the interview *I never open my mouth!* So many salesman come in to see me, hand me something to read, and when I start to read, *they keep right on talking!* So I stop reading and look at the salesman until he gets through talking . . . then I start reading again. *But he begins talking again!*

(I always feel like saying: "Well, now, look! What do you want me to do? Do you want me to read this, or do you want me to listen to you?")

Mr. Bowers lay there on the sofa and read his Estate Analysis completely through, without a word.

When he finished, he dropped it alongside of him on the floor indifferently and said nothing.

I waited a few moments, then asked: "How do you like it?"

BOWERS. I don't *want* any life insurance.

ME. Why?

BOWERS. I've told you from the first time you came in to see me, *I don't believe* in life insurance! (*He suddenly got hot. I knew I had a fight on my hands. My job was to bring him to life. I wasn't being scared off, because I knew I was on the right track.*)

ME. Mr. Bowers, *in addition to that,* isn't there some other reason why you have never bought life insurance?

BOWERS. No. That's all. I just don't believe in life insurance!

ME (*Pause*). Mr. Bowers, there is a statement I wish to make. I want you to distinctly understand that, as the result of this interview, you are not going to be asked to buy any life insurance. In order for you to feel perfectly free to answer any questions that I may ask, or to ask any questions *you* wish, I am not going to ask you to buy when we are finished. Is that satisfactory?

BOWERS. O.K. Go ahead.

ME (*I drew my chair closer to him and held the Balance Sheet in such a position that we could both look at it. At the bottom of the page it read: "Additional Capital I Need to Meet My Requirements"* . . . $156,600 *Pointing to the first item, at the top of the page, I said:*) Mr. Bowers, you frankly admitted that if anything were to happen to you, your wife would need a minimum income of $700 a month. Do you recall that?

BOWERS. That's right.

ME. At first, you set that figure at $1,000 a month, but later you agreed to let me cut that down to $700 a month, isn't that right?

BOWERS. Yes.

ME. Now yourself, at Age 60. You told me you would like to be in a position to retire at 60, and $700 a month income would be the least you would want to retire on. Is that right?

BOWERS. I'll have more than that.

ME. You told me that if anything happens and you should become disabled and unable to work, you couldn't get along on less than $700 a month. Is that correct?

BOWERS. Yes, but I'm not going to become disabled.

ME. But a guaranteed income of $700 a month in the event of your disability would be a tremendous help to you, wouldn't it?

BOWERS. Oh, sure.

ME. You frankly told me, if you were going to assume the responsibility that Mrs. Bowers must assume in the event of your untimely death, you would have to have this $700 a month income until John and your baby Katharine were twenty-one, didn't you?

BOWERS. I don't want any life insurance.

ME. Mr. Bowers, I am in a position to do something for you this afternoon that no other living person can do for you.

BOWERS. What's that?

ME (*Producing two policies*). On the strength of the splendid examination you passed, I took the privilege of having these contracts issued without any obligation on your part. These contracts (*handing them to him*) you can immediately put into your wife's safe deposit box, the equivalent of money saved in bonds, if you lived and saved for twenty years.

BOWERS. How much do they cost?

ME. They cost you *nothing*. It's an investment. It's merely a transfer of bank balances. You simply transfer $3,418 from that $20,000 bank balance (*pointing to the Cash On Hand item on the Balance Sheet*) to your insurance bank balance, and you have automatically, *this minute,* fulfilled the objectives you set for yourself and your family whether you live, or die, or become disabled.

BOWERS. Leave these policies with me and I'll think it over.

ME. That's part of my job, to *help* you think it over. You don't have to think over the physical examination or the inspection report. That's already been done. You don't have to think over whether you need this protection in the event of your disability, do you?

BOWERS. No.

ME. You don't have to think over whether your wife needs this income of $700 a month, do you?

BOWERS. There are lots of other things to think about.

ME. May I just say this: You would do this in a moment if Mrs. Bowers were earning the money instead of you, wouldn't you? If you knew that everything you have would be taken away from you if she died, you would certainly do this, wouldn't you?

BOWERS. *I told you I am not going to buy any life insurance.*

ME (*Ours is a business with much emotion. If a prospect can't get emotional over the fact that his family is faced with disaster,* I believe it is up to us to get emotional for him! *This was one of those times when I didn't have to begin to feel emotional, I already was emotional! I knew his wife was back there listening. I got up and paced back and forth across the room*). Mr. Bowers (*I said it without much effort to control my feelings*), did you ever hear of a *blitzkrieg*?

BOWERS (*Really coming to life for the first time*). Yes.

ME. Do you know what a *blitzkrieg* is?

BOWERS. Sure.

ME. Well, if anything happens to you, it's going to be a *blitzkrieg* for your family! Would you want your little boy and your baby girl to be without this income if you and Mrs. Bowers were both taken away?

BOWERS (*There was a long silence. I was standing over at the front window looking out. Finally, I heard him say quietly:*) How much do the premiums on these policies amount to?

(*I went over to him, took the policies, added the figures and they came to the exact sum I had in the Estate Analysis. I showed him.*)

BOWERS (*Calling to his wife*). Katharine! *Bring me my checkbook.*

10.

*Analysis of the Basic
Sales Principles
Used in Making That Sale*

L ET'S ANALYZE that sale. How can *you* use this technique? It sells insurance, but how can you use it in selling "shoes or ships or sealing-wax"?

Without going into all the fundamentals such as the advantage of making appointments, being prepared, key issue, etc., so obvious in this interview:

> I always have a heavy X penciled where the prospect signs. I hand him my pen, and pointing to the large X, say in a routine manner: *"Right here."* Sometimes I say: *"Will you write your name here the same as I have filled it in at the top."* I try to have the application form previously filled in, or at least have his name and address at the top. There is some sort of strange psychology back of this. I've never been quite sure what it is, but it makes the close easier for both the buyer and the salesman.

MAGIC PHRASES

"That's entirely all right. You are to be the sole judge of that."
People don't like to be sold. They like to buy. So I always assume the role of "Assistant Buyer." However, in that position, I feel it is my duty to produce all the evidence!

"Why?"
The most powerful word in the English language! I use *"Why?"* and *"Why not?"* frequently in practically every interview.

"In addition to that, Mr. Bowers, isn't there something else—some other reason that makes you hesitate to go ahead with this plan?"
A man generally has two reasons for not doing a thing—one that sounds good . . . and a *real* one. Keeping records for years, I found that it's two to one he doesn't give you the real one the first time. The best formula I ever found to draw out the *real* one is built around those two little questions *"Why?"* and *"In addition to that . . . ?"*

"Mr. Bowers, there is a statement I wish to make. I want you to distinctly understand that, as the result of this interview, you are not going to be asked to buy. In order for you to feel perfectly free to answer any questions that I may ask, or to ask any questions YOU *wish, I am not going to ask you to buy when we are finished. Is that satisfactory?"*
(Let me say: I never *ask* a man to buy. There is only one way I've found to get anybody to do anything.

That goes whether it's my own children or any other person. And that is by making him want to do it!)

"Additional Capital I Need to Meet My Requirements"

These magic words are right in my questionnaire, remember? And then the words, *"set by you."* My whole sale revolves around this. If I have done a good information-getting job, if my facts are correct, this eliminates most of the objections usually raised. There are the prospect's assets and liabilities. One of the chief of all objections, "I can't afford it," seldom comes up. . . . We can always afford the things we *want!*

"I am in a position to do something for you this afternoon that no other living person can do for you."

A powerful, motivating phrase! Where it honestly fits, it has surprising effect.

"That's part of my job, to help you think it over. You don't have to think over the . . ." (then back to your *questions* to find out just what it is he wants to think over).

"Mr. Bowers, did you ever hear of a blitzkrieg?"

It is often necessary to arouse people and stir them to action for their own benefit. Basically, there are only two factors that move men to action: *desire for gain,* and *fear of loss. Fear* is the most motivating factor where risk or danger is involved. . . .

"Would you want your little boy and your baby girl to be without this income if you and Mrs. Bowers were both taken away?"

Put YOU in the interview: I was surprised to find in analyzing this sale, that I had used the word "you" or "yours" sixty-six times. I don't remember where I first heard of this test, but it is a superb way for you to make certain you are practicing the most important rule of all:

See things from the other person's point of view and talk in terms of his wants, needs, and desires!

Do you want to try a highly profitable test on yourself? Write out what you said in your last selling interview. Then see in how many places you can strike out the personal pronoun "I" or "we" and change it to "you" or "yours." Put YOU in the interview.

There is an old saying: The salesman who sells only to the man who is ready to buy will not make money enough to pay his railroad fare.

One of the most important turning points in my career was when I heard one of America's topflight salesmen, J. Elliott Hall of New York City, reveal an amazing method of meeting objections—not with smart stock answers found in books written about "How To Meet Objections." He met those objections by *asking questions*. He didn't attempt to tell his objectors that they were wrong, and show them how much smarter he was than they. He simply asked questions that added up to just *one* conclusion . . . a sound conclusion based on facts.

The profound lesson I learned from that master salesman changed my whole way of thinking. He never gave the impression that he was trying to persuade or influence anybody to *his* way of thinking. Elliott Hall's questions had only one purpose:

To help the other fellow recognize what he wants—what he really wants—then help him decide how to get it!

In the final interview with Mr. Bowers, I asked him eighteen questions. Glance back over a few of them. I think you will agree that, if I had attempted to say *exactly* the same things to him without putting them in the form of questions, I'd have been kicked out in three minutes flat!

I will not review these same questions again, but you will recognize them in other interviews later. I have counted a total of fifty-six "magic phrases" in this book which I will point out as we go along. Most of them you can use almost verbatim in selling *anything*. Many that relate strictly to insurance may easily be translated and adapted for selling and dealing with people anywhere at any time.

AN IDEA I LEARNED IN BASEBALL THAT I HAVE USED EVERY DAY IN SELLING

After the game one day in St. Louis, when I was playing with the Cardinals, Roger Bresnahan, our manager, said to me: "I want to see you here tomorrow morning at ten o'clock—in uniform!"

It was the middle of July, long after morning practice was discontinued, and I wondered what he had in mind.

Let me tell you what happened that following morning out on the diamond:

Five players were there in uniform: a catcher, batter, first baseman, second baseman, and myself at shortstop. But I seemed to be the only one the manager was working on. While the batter hit ground balls to my left and to my right, Bresnahan stood back of me, watching. I picked up each ball and threw it to first, then we'd throw the ball around the diamond a couple of times to each other.

I thought, "What goes on here? Why has he got us out here in all this heat?"

Pretty soon he said: "Frank, you've got a bad habit of playing the ball on your side. Try to get in front of every ball. *Play 'em straight in front of you!*"

I started to give him an argument. But he cut me off sharp—"Listen! Do you want to play on this ball club?"

"Sure," I replied.

"All right then. You do what I tell you, and we won't have any trouble!"

We went on with that rehearsal for some time. Sure enough, to my surprise, I found that playing 'em straight in front of me made fielding much easier, and more sure. If the ball took a bad hop, I was in a better position to shift either way. A couple of them hopped up—hit me in the chest—I grabbed the ball quickly and threw it to first. Bresnahan was pleased.

After I became convinced how right he was, I asked him where he first got this idea. "From the greatest brain that ever played baseball," declared Roger. *"John McGraw!"*

Later, I had a chance to ask the famous John Mc-Graw himself about this. He said, "That's right. Whether it's a ground ball, thrown ball, or fly ball—never take it on the side if you can get in front of it. *Play 'em straight in front of you!"*

Years later, I discovered that this same principle applied to selling. It happened one day when I was trying to interview a busy executive. He was one of those "forty minute eggs" who wouldn't look at me as he talked. Suddenly I seemed to hear Roger Bresnahan's voice: "PLAY 'EM STRAIGHT IN FRONT OF YOU!"

I moved casually around in front of my man, and began looking straight into his face with eager, absorbed interest. The effect was *magic!* What started out as a quick "brush-off" interview developed into one of the best and most exciting interviews I ever had. I left there with all the information I needed, which enabled me to open up a large sale on this man, and the other three officers of his company.

Practically every time I talk with anyone I think of Roger Bresnahan and the importance of the principle he taught me that hot July morning out on the ball diamond. Whether it's a sitting or a standing interview, I try to face a man straight ahead. If I can't get in front of him, I turn my head so that I am looking straight into his face.

I have had men talk two and three hours after saying they were "too busy to talk with salesmen"; and tell me intimate, private things they never told anybody before.

I believe people usually judge you by the way you act and react toward them. When I listen with undivided attention, I get excited and become enthusiastic —just the same as when *I'm* doing the talking. Then, I notice the *other* person usually becomes more enthusiastic.

Now that I've reached the age where I'm looking back, trying to discover the reason for things that did the most for me, I realize more than ever the importance of this simple little rule I first learned over forty years ago, "PLAY 'EM STRAIGHT IN FRONT OF YOU!"

PART THREE

The Most Profound Secret of Successful Selling, and How I Learned to Apply It

11.

The One Big Secret of Success

DURING THE WORST PERIOD of a nationwide depression, a young man just graduating from a large eastern university applied for a position in a big department store located in the same city. He carried with him a letter of introduction from his father to the president, an old classmate of his at college.

The president read the letter then said to the young man: "I wish I *could* give you a position. Your father was one of my best friends in college, and every year I look forward to seeing him again at our class reunions. But, unfortunately, you have come to me at the worst possible time. Our business has been losing money so long, we have been compelled to lay off every employee except the most important people in our organization."

Many other graduating students from the college applied to the same store for a position. And they were all told the same story.

So, when still another student remarked one day that he was going there for a job, they laughed and told him he would be wasting his time.

But that didn't discourage this young fellow. *He had an idea!* When he walked into that big department store, he had no letter of introduction. He went directly to the president's office, but he didn't ask for a job. In fact, he didn't say anything about what *he* wanted. He sent a note in to the president about something the *president* wanted! The note read: "I've got an idea that will help your store get out of the depression. May I tell you about it?"

"Send him in!" ordered the head of the store.

Coming immediately to the point, the young man said: "I want to help you open a College Department. We would handle nothing but clothes for college men! There are 16,000 students in our college, their number is increasing every year. I don't know anything about buying clothes, but I do know what those boys like. Let me have one of your good buyers, and I'll help you set up the kind of department the students will like. Then I'll *sell* them the idea and get them coming in here."

In a short time, that store had a brand new kind of department which quickly became the livest and one of the most profitable the store ever had!

Back in the days when I was groping around in the dark, desperately trying to learn how to sell, I unknowingly used this same principle and it resulted in one of the biggest individual sales ever made in my company. Later, I was congratulated by one of the country's foremost salesmen who told me something that I soon learned was the *most profound secret of dealing with people!*

Said he: "I still doubt whether you understand exactly *why* you were able to make that sale."

I asked him what he meant.

He then uttered the most vital truth I have ever heard about selling. He said: "The most important secret of salesmanship is *to find out what the other fellow wants, then help him find the best way to get it.* That man you sold didn't want life insurance. *Nobody* wants life insurance! In the first minute of your interview, you took a blind stab, and accidentally found what he *did* want. Then you showed him *how* he could get it. You kept on talking more about it, and asking more questions about it, never letting him get away from the thing *he* wanted. If you will always remember this one rule, selling will be easy."

What this great salesman said made such a profound impression on me I could think of little else for days. I soon realized with full force how valuable a lesson I had learned. I resolved to dedicate the rest of my selling career to this principle:

Finding out what people want, and helping them get it!

I can't begin to tell you the new kind of courage and enthusiasm this gave me. Here was something more than a sales technique. It was a philosophy to live by.

12.

Applying This Principle
Raised Them from Small Jobbers
to Big Construction Engineers

I CALLED ONE TIME on a young firm of building contractors who occupied a third floor back room of an old residence near the center of the city. There were two partners, one of them a young man of twenty-seven. He was alone in the office at the time, typing out an estimate for a bid on a small job.

After the usual routine approach, I got the "green light" and I began talking to him about his future and the future of his business.

In a few minutes, he interrupted me. "Listen," he laughed, "you're wasting your time. You are talking so far over our heads, it's funny! We started this business on a shoestring, and we only do small alteration jobs. We can't bid on big jobs."

ME. Why?
HIM. We don't have the money.
ME. How long have you been in business?
HIM. Two years.
ME. How do you plan to get enough money to bid on big jobs?
HIM. I don't know. Maybe we'll get a break sometime.
ME. How did you get started in the building business?
HIM. My partner and I worked for a big builder. He made a lot of money, then got to drinking. Tom and I saw that we

weren't getting anywhere, so one day I said: "Tom, what do you say you and I go into business for ourselves?"

ME: How old is Tom?

HIM. Thirty-seven.

ME. Has he got any ability? (*I then listened to the most enthusiastic eulogy I ever heard one partner give about another, both as to ability and character.*) Could you repeat that story to a banker friend of mine—*exactly* the way you just told it to me?

HIM. Sure!

ME. Good! What you need is *credit*. I think I can help you establish credit at the bank, so that you can bid on big contracts. There are two steps to the plan: First—I want to have you and your partner examined by our doctor to establish your insurability. Second—If you are both approved for life insurance, then I want to make an appointment for all three of us to see a banker friend of mine. Is that satisfactory?

HIM. That's O.K. with me.

ME. Where can I see Tom? I want to meet him.

. . . Twenty minutes later, I was interviewing Tom on the roof of a building where he was supervising an alteration job. He was a big fellow, with an honest, friendly manner, and a wonderful, warmhearted smile. He really looked the part his younger partner claimed for him.

He was busy, but I repeated very briefly my interview with his partner, and told him I was so much impressed by his partner's enthusiasm that I believed I could help them.

TOM. How do you mean you can help us?

ME. (*I then repeated my two-step plan for them.*)

TOM. Did Joe agree to this?

ME. Yes. And he sent me here to tell you about my plan.

The following morning, both partners were examined. I had $100,000 issued in four $25,000 Ordinary Life policies. The morning I laid those policies down in front of them at their office, they burst out laughing and shook all over, laughing so hard they could hardly stop. One of them was carrying $1,000.

The other $5,000. And both were paying premiums on a quarterly basis.

One hundred thousand looked like a *million* to them. For a while they couldn't believe I was serious.

I said, "Am I serious? Here's how serious I am. I'm going to put this $100,000 in force *right now!* When we keep this appointment with the banker, I want you to have these policies with you."

Tom (*Laughing*). How are we going to pay for them?

Me. You are going to pay for them easier than you find it now to pay for these little policies you've already got. *You are going to get some big jobs!*

They gave me a small deposit that morning for the annual premiums on that $100,000, and signed notes for the balance, payable in three months. I explained that the notes would be renewed from time to time, until they were able to pay them in full. I promised that if they failed to get any big contracts, the notes would be returned to them, and they could tear them up . . . they would owe me nothing. "I've got so much confidence in you two men, I am willing to take this risk," I assured them.

The next day, the three of us met in the office of the vice-president of a large bank. We had an appointment. My instructions were for the big fellow to remain silent, but give my banker friend his *best* smile. My only fear was that the younger partner wouldn't repeat his story about Tom with the same exciting enthusiasm that he had when he first told it to me.

Well . . . he did even *better!* He gave several examples of big jobs Tom handled for their old boss. He spoke with enthusiasm and conviction. Anyone could see this young builder was sincere and believed every word he said. When the banker asked about the amount of insurance they carried, he produced the four policies totalling $100,000.

Those young men succeeded in establishing a line of credit with the bank which made it possible for them to start bidding on big contracts.

Praise, confidence, and honest appreciation of one man for

another, enabled them to start in business on a shoestring, and within a few years become one of the largest and best-known construction engineering concerns in the city of Philadelphia.

Finally, they built their life insurance up to a total of nearly a *million dollars*. Naturally, I got all this business—and a lot more—because they became a great center of influence for me.

They often said, however, that no insurance they ever bought —not even the big building contracts they landed later—gave them the thrill of that first $100,000 I sold them the morning they thought the whole thing must be a big joke!

Can you imagine how far I would have got if I had gone in there with merely selling insurance to those men as my sole objective?

Applying this principle: *Finding out what they wanted, then talking in terms of trying to help them get it,* made it possible for me to hit a home run with the bases full.

13.

*His Chief Objection
Was a Buying Signal!*

DURING THE WORST PERIOD of a depression, I was
walking down Broad Street in Philadelphia with a friend
of mine. As we passed an open-air parking lot, our attention
was attracted by two fellows who I thought were wrestling. A
small crowd was beginning to gather. I said to my friend, "Bill,
what's going on there?" Bill laughed. "Don't you know?" he
answered. "That big fellow is putting the other fellow into a
strait jacket. Watch the little guy demonstrate to the crowd
how to get out!"

While we stopped for a few minutes to watch him, it struck
me that many of us salesmen were in a "strait jacket" due to
the depression—especially veterans in the business—and we didn't
know how to get out! I had been in one myself recently, and
my production had hit a new low.

As I saw that little fellow easily slide out of what looked like
an impossible situation, without attempting to force or break
any part of the jacket, the thought occurred to me: "The only
way you can get out of your strait jacket, Bettger, is to find a
method of presenting plans that will appeal *because* of present
day conditions!"

Later that day, I phoned a man whose name had been given
to me by a friend of mine, Jack Howard. My friend had said,
"This man is president of a comparatively new business. He has
put all his money into the company, but he'll make a big success of it. They are pretty well established now, but this is only

the beginning. It's going to develop into something *really* big! I don't know anything about his insurance, but he should be a good prospect—only thirty-eight years old."

I had made several previous attempts to see him, without any luck. But that afternoon I reached him on the telephone. I told him I was a friend of Jack Howard, that I had written him a letter about three weeks ago, but was unable to contact him on the phone, and had found he was out of town a great deal.

He said, "Mr. Bettger, it is humanly impossible for me to keep pace with everything. It's a tremendous job getting this business organized. I don't want to be short with you, but there is absolutely no chance to sell me insurance, even if I *did* see you. I am carrying more than my present income justifies. The fact is I don't know how I can meet the payments on about $100,000 that I already have. It would be a total waste of time to talk about any additional insurance."

I didn't doubt anything he said, and I felt it would be futile to talk further about an appointment, so I said: "Mr. Raymond, what I really want to talk to you about is your *business*. I understand you are putting tremendous effort into your organization, which is practically a new business. You are giving your time to it day and night, isn't that right?"

"Yes, and seven days a week right now," he answered.

"And you have put a lot of money into it, I suppose?"

"Just about everything I've got," he admitted.

"Well, I'm sure you have done a wise thing," I said. "The best investment a man can make is in his *own* business. I've been told by people who ought to know that you are going to make a big success of it *if you live*. But, Mr. Raymond, if you should die before you get this business fully established, don't you think it would be a highly speculative investment for your family? You wouldn't leave instructions for your executor or trustee to invest your widow's money in that kind of investment, would you?"

"That's why I'm trying to hold onto all this insurance I am already carrying," he explained.

"You are taking as little salary out of the business as you possibly can, I suppose, aren't you?"

"That's right," he agreed. (Every question I asked, I was afraid he was going to ask me to excuse him, that he was too busy to talk. Instead, I now sensed that he wanted to find out what I was leading up to.)

"So you have put all your money into this new company. Your services are worth far more than the salary you are drawing. For the next few years, the success or failure of this business depends on *you*. Your death would mean a loss to your business, your associates, and to your family. To your wife and your children, it is a loss because your salary stops *immediately*. They couldn't sell or even borrow on your shares of stock which they would inherit . . . and the chances of dividends being paid for some time are quite uncertain, isn't that right?"

"That's right," he agreed.

"This *always* brings distress to a man's family, and in turn causes great pressure, legal and otherwise, upon those who are left to run the business. Don't you think, Mr. Raymond, that both sides at interest deserve every possible protection?"

"That's the risk I knew I had to take for a few years until we become completely organized," he declared.

"Why should *you* take that risk for a few years—or even a few *days?*" I asked. "Suppose you should wake up tonight, in the middle of the night, and it should suddenly occur to you that the fire insurance on that big building you bought last year had expired yesterday. You probably wouldn't be able to get back to sleep the rest of the night! And the first thing tomorrow morning you would have your broker on the phone telling him to protect you immediately, wouldn't you?"

"Yes, I suppose I would."

"Yet, Mr. Raymond, only one building out of seven *ever* burns. Isn't it a hundred times more important that your corporation immediately insure your life and *transfer the Big risk to the insurance companies?*"

"Now you are talking about something interesting," he said.

"We *may* consider something like that. I'll talk to my business associates about it."

"Don't do that," I said. "That is my job. It might be embarrassing for you to tell them how important you are to the business, and that the corporation should insure your life so that your family can get *your* money out of the business if anything happens to *you*. Coming from you, it may seem selfish. I can do it better than you can. But before I talk to them, I want to make sure my company would be willing to pay out a large sum in case of your death. I want to have my doctor come over and establish your insurability."

"All right, you may do that," he agreed willingly. "I am going out of town tonight, but you can have your doctor see me here in my office on Thursday morning."

14.

How I Learned to Get Faster and More Favorable Action from My Company

ONE OF THE FIRST big sales I made was for $100,000 on a man who had just been made president of his company. Incidentally, I never would have heard of him if I hadn't asked for names from a man I had just sold. He then recalled the recent promotion of his friend.

Well, when the $100,000 was approved and the policy issued, *was I excited!* This man's company was buying the insurance for their own protection, so I was sure I could sell an extra twenty-five or fifty to the man personally.

I phoned his office for an appointment, but his secretary said the president had been out of town for a couple of days and was expected back in the office the next morning. She said she was sure it would be all right if I came down first thing in the morning.

The next day, just as I started to leave my desk, my phone rang: "Is that you, Frank?" . . . I recognized the voice immediately. It was R. F. Tull, Secretary of my company and head of the Department of Issue. Instantly, I knew by the tone of his voice something was wrong.

"Frank, have you delivered that $100,000 policy on Robinson yet?"

Like a flash, something told me to say "Yes." But I paused, before I could answer. Then, somehow, I managed to say, "No,

I haven't, Mr. Tull. I was just this minute leaving to go down and deliver it."

"Frank, I'm glad you didn't," he said. "I wish you would hold it for a couple of days. Some information has just come to us this morning that sounds pretty bad. I hope it's not correct for *your* sake, and for ours, too, but if it is, we just can't let this man have that insurance."

"What's wrong?" I asked, beginning to feel sick all over.

"Frank, I'm not at liberty to disclose the information," said Mr. Tull. "It was given to us in the strictest confidence. But let me assure you we are going to double check it immediately to make absolutely certain whether it is authentic."

"Mr. Tull, would you feel better if I returned the contract for you to hold?" My voice actually trembled.

"Frank," said he earnestly, "that is mighty decent. If you do that, we won't forget your fairness to co-operate with us."

. . . Well, that case never was approved. It took the wind out of my sails for quite awhile. Frankly, I had figured up my commission, and already had spent some of it. The loss, at that time, was a hard blow for me to take.

However, over the years, I'm sure I didn't lose anything. I learned later that life insurance companies give agents a "rating." As a result my company gave me a "preferred" rating. And I have always tried to preserve it.

Another thing I've found: Most companies love to get letters from their salesmen, attached to the order, giving them all the information they can. This frequently saves time and expense. The salesman usually is familiar with information and facts that might be impossible for the company to obtain through the usual channels.

Let me repeat! The loss of that big sale taught me *two lessons* which have helped me get faster and more favorable action from my company—right down to the present day:

1. *Get a check with the order.* I could have got a check with the order in this sale if I had asked for it. But I was afraid. If I had, the moment that contract was issued, it automatically would have be-

come effective and Mr. Tull couldn't have recalled
it.

2. *Get all the information you can, and be careful to
   get it as accurately as possible.* Most of this, I found,
   I could get in the fact-finding interview. After closing the sale, if I need more facts, I say: "Mr. Rob-
   inson, I've found that it's smart to attach a letter to
   the application. You know more about your affairs than anybody else can possibly know. My letter to the company saves time, and frequently eliminates much of the personal investigation usually
   necessary."

15.

The Deal Before the Deal

HAVE YOU EVER given a valuable idea to a prospect, yet failed to make the sale because he wanted to give his business to a friend, or someone else he was accustomed to deal with?

Have you ever had a prospective buyer encourage you, draw you out for information, figures, get your ideas about his situation; only to find out later that you never had a chance for the sale?

I don't mean to criticize any buyer for doing this. We all realize this is common practice, probably more frequently encountered in the sale of tangibles than intangibles.

I had this happen to me many times until I found a simple little phrase which frequently has the effect of placing me on an equal plane with my competitor. Let me give you one example:

I called on the president and principal owner of a large electrical contracting concern. I had a letter of introduction to him. Here is the interview:

MR. BROWN. I'm sorry, you're a little late. I just agreed to take a Retirement Income Policy that will pay me $____ a month, starting when I reach Age 60. I want to quit this grind and start doing the things I want to do before I get too old to enjoy them.

ME. You are a very wise man. There is only one thing you will ever regret about it.

BROWN. What's that?

ME. The income isn't enough. You ought to make it twice as much.

Brown. No. I don't want to start something I can't go through with. This will cost me about $_____ a year. And I've already got quite a bit of insurance right now.

Me. What company are you going to buy this in? Would you mind telling me?

Brown. The "X" Mutual.

Me. That is a great company. You couldn't possibly go wrong with them.

Brown. Yes, I understand they are one of the best. I already have a couple of policies with them. The agent is a friend of mine.

Me. Where were you born, Mr. Brown—in Philadelphia?

Brown. No, I was born in Hartford, Connecticut.

Me. Oh, is that so? Hartford is the great insurance city, you know. Would you mind telling me your date of birth?

Brown. May 17, 1927.

Me. Well, did you know that your insurable age will advance from forty-two to forty-three in a couple of days?

Brown. Yes. That's the reason I just signed up to get in under Age 42.

Me. Have you been examined yet by the doctor?

Brown. Not yet.

Me. Have you given them your check?

Brown. No. Why?

Me. *If I give you an idea, will I benefit by it?*

Brown. What do you mean?

Me. Did you say you want to quit this grind before you get too old to enjoy doing the things you want to do?

Brown. That's right.

Me. If I can show you how you can quit the grind a year earlier, yet cost you *less* money . . . will you give me the business?

Brown (*Looking very skeptical*). How can you do that?

Me. I think I can. Are you interested?

Brown. Yes.

Me. *It's a deal!* Let's lay our cards right out on the table. Have you got your "X" Mutual proposal here?

Brown. Yes. I have it.

ME. Good. Let's put it on the table. And *you* are to be the sole judge. Right?

BROWN (*Pulled the proposal out of his desk and laid it face up on the table.*)

ME (*I took one quick glance. That's all I needed.*) I can give you exactly the same contract, Mr. Brown, producing the same results, but your income—$___ a month—will start twelve months before!

BROWN. And it won't cost me more money?

ME. It will cost you *less* money!

BROWN. What's the joker?

ME. There is no joker (*pulling out my rate book*). Here's all you do. Instead of buying your insurance at Age 42, we date your application the day *after* your insurable age advances to Age 43. Then, instead of making 18 payments for 18 years, you only make 17 payments for 17 years! That saves you money. But what is even more important, your income starts twelve months *earlier!* (*As I spoke, I drew this little diagram.*)

Age 42	*18 payments*	*60½*	*$___ Month for life*
Age 43	*17 payments*	*59½*	*$___ Month for life*

In other words, you retire and begin to really live and enjoy life *an entire year earlier!* How do you like it?

Mr. Brown was astounded. He said, "Well, here is one time when it pays to buy your insurance at the *older* age, is that right?"

"That is right," I said smiling, at the same time casually withdrawing an application from my pocket. "What is your wife's full name, Mr. Brown?"

. . . After Mr. Brown signed the application and handed me his check, he said: "Well, *you win* . . . but let me ask you a question. Why didn't the 'X' Mutual man tell me about this?"

"For the same reason that I lost a sale several years ago under the same circumstances. He probably doesn't know about it."

MAGIC PHRASES

"If I give you an idea, will I benefit by it?"
Note: The critical turning point in that interview
started when I asked that question.

I make the deal *before* revealing the idea. In other
words, I think of it as—

The Deal Before The Deal!

16.

I Lost the Sale,
But Gained Something Far More
Valuable Than the Commission
I Would Have Made

AS I WAS ABOUT to leave the president of a large roller-bearing manufacturing company one day, I said: "Mr. Jordon, you must have some promising young men here in your organization. If one of them walked into your office right now, you wouldn't hesitate to introduce me, would you?"

"No, of course not," he replied.

I pulled out a few of my 4″ by 2½″ cards of introduction, handed him one and said: "Can you think of one of these young men right now?"

He filled out two, and then said: "By the way, there's a fine young fellow in the next office; he asked my advice about some insurance just the other day. But I told him I didn't know enough about it to advise him. Would you want to talk to him if I call him in?"

"I'd like very much to talk with him," I replied.

The president pressed the buzzer for his secretary and told her to send for Mr. Taylor.

Mr. Taylor really was a fine-looking young man. Mr. Jordon introduced us, then said, "John, have you done anything about that insurance yet?"

"No, I haven't, Mr. Jordon."

"Mr. Bettger is a life insurance man. I just bought some more from him. I thought while he was here, you might like to ask his advice about your problem." The young man looked pleased and said, "Yes sir, I'd like to."

I said, "I'll try to help you, Mr. Taylor. Tell me all about it."

"Well," he explained, "an old fellow came out here about three weeks ago. I don't know how he got my name. He told me all about a policy that he said was just right for me. Finally, I agreed to let him send his doctor out to examine me with the understanding that there would be no obligation. He said it would give me a chance to see the policy itself, then I could decide better whether I wanted it. Well, the doctor came the next morning, and about a week later, the old fellow came here with the policy. He wanted me to take it right then, but I wanted to look it over awhile. He keeps calling up, but each time I tell him I haven't been able to decide yet, and I'll let him know later."

"Do you have the policy here?" I asked.

"Yes, I have," he nodded.

"Why don't you bring it right in here," suggested the president in a kindly way.

While he was gone, Mr. Jordon said, "I think if you sell him the same thing I just bought, he'll be . . ."

Just then young Taylor came back with the policy and handed it to me. "You see, Mr. Bettger, I don't know this old fellow, and I don't know anything about the company."

They both watched me as I unfolded the contract. I sensed a very easy sale.

It was a $10,000 Twenty Payment Life contract in the Mutual Life of New York written as of Age 26. Young Taylor's age had since changed and his insurable age was now twenty-seven. His wife was named beneficiary if living, otherwise children of the insured.

Nothing was said while I looked the contract over.

"Do you have any children, Mr. Taylor?" I asked.

"Yes. A little boy, a year and a half."

"According to your application here, you have no other insurance. Is that correct?"

"Yes. That is right," he admitted.

"What are you waiting for?" I asked.

"What do you mean?" Taylor asked, looking puzzled.

"You want my honest advice, don't you?"

"Yes . . . sure."

"Knowing what I do about the life insurance business," I said, "if you were my own younger brother, I'd tell you to get that old fellow on the telephone as quickly as you can, and tell him to put this insurance in force as soon as possible."

Both the young man and the president looked completely surprised. Mr. Jordon spoke up: "Why do you say that, Mr. Bettger? Isn't that a pretty expensive form of policy for a young man twenty-six to buy?"

"Mr. Jordon, if there ever was a *right* time to buy Twenty Payment Life, I'd say Age 26 was it. I've never heard of anyone who regretted buying a Twenty Payment Life," I declared.

"What about the company?" asked Taylor.

"None better in the world," I answered, "and did you know that the Mutual Life of New York is the oldest life insurance company in America?"

"Is that so?" said the president.

"I could tell you that I can do better for you, but the truth is I can't do as well," I admitted.

"Why not?" asked young Taylor.

"Because this Mutual Life man is in a position to do something for you that no other living person can do for you," I said, grinning. "He is in a position to put $10,000 of insurance in force on your life *this minute!* If I tried to insure you, first I'd have to get you examined. There's a possibility that another doctor *might* find something wrong. If he did, the Mutual Life would immediately withdraw their policy. Even if I did get you through without any trouble, the best I could do would be to insure you as of Age 27, instead of twenty-six."

. . . Shortly after this happened, Clayt Hunsicker, who was president that year of the Philadelphia Association of Life

Underwriters, said to me: "Frank, an old fellow named Joe Doakes with the Mutual Life told me something yesterday. He said he had a $10,000 policy out on inspection with a prospect for a couple of weeks and had just given up all hope of delivering it when the prospect called him on the phone and told him to come right out and get a check—that another life insurance man had advised him to do it.

"Frank," said Clayt, "that was a fine thing for you to do. Joe hasn't been well enough to work much for some time. That poor devil really needs the money. He broke down and cried when he told me about what you'd done."

I am not a C.L.U., but I have tried to follow their code, conceived and written by Solomon S. Huebner, President Emeritus, American College of Chartered Life Underwriters. I have profited richly by following it. Any salesman would profit by adopting it:

> In all my relations with clients, I agree to observe the following rule of professional conduct: I shall in the light of all the circumstances surrounding my client, which I shall make every effort to ascertain and understand, give him that service, which, had I been in the same circumstances, I would have applied to myself.

17.

A Magic Phrase That Helps Men Raise Their Sights

I WAS REFERRED one time to a wholesale coal dealer. He started to interview me standing up in the outer office. There was a low rail partition between us as we talked:

EARNSHAW. I'm sorry. You're just a little late. I signed up with the Travelers a couple of days ago for $25,000.

ME. Congratulations. You picked out a wonderful company.

EARNSHAW (*looking pleased*). Do you think so?

ME. None better in the world. . . . What kind of policy did you buy, Mr. Earnshaw?

EARNSHAW. Twenty Payment Life.

ME. Well, you'll never regret buying that.

EARNSHAW (*looking more pleased*). It sounds good to me. I pay $1,025 a year. If I die, they pay my estate $25,000. In twenty years, my policy is full paid; or, if I want my money back, they return to me *almost every dollar I paid them!*

ME. You'd wonder how they can do it, wouldn't you?

EARNSHAW. Yes, you would. *I* don't know how they can do it.

ME. Mr. Earnshaw, would you mind telling me how much life insurance you've got, altogether?

EARNSHAW. This brings me up to $75,000 . . . No, $76,000.

ME. *Good.* You know something? *You'll never be satisfied until you get it up to $100,000.*

EARNSHAW. Yes, I suppose so.

ME. How old are you, Mr. Earnshaw?

EARNSHAW. Forty-six.

ME. I'll tell you what I can do for you. For $412 I can bring your insurance up to $100,000 right now!

EARNSHAW. How do you mean?

ME. For only $412 I can get you an additional $25,000.

EARNSHAW. How?

ME. May I come in for a few minutes?

EARNSHAW (*reached down and unlatched the rail gate*). Come in.

ME (*after we were seated in his private office*). Have the Travelers approved you for this $25,000?

EARNSHAW. I think so. The agent called me on the phone this morning and said the doctor's examination was O.K.

ME. *Fine!* Now, while you are able to pass, I can get you an additional $25,000 in the Fidelity Mutual on the Five Year Term Plan. Any time during the five years, you may convert it to the Twenty Payment Plan, or any other plan, *without* a medical re-examination. This puts you in the driver's seat. (*As I spoke, I deliberately removed the application from my pocket, unfolded it, and laid it on Mr. Earnshaw's desk, directly in front of him. There was the large X on the dotted line where he was to sign.*)

EARNSHAW. (*As he read, I removed my fountain pen from my pocket, adjusted it for writing, but sat there quietly. He read through most of the questions. When he turned and looked at me, I handed him my pen.*)

ME. Right here. (*I touched my finger on the dotted line.*)

EARNSHAW (*signed his name without a word*).

ME. Do you want to give me a check for the full year, Mr. Earnshaw, or would you rather just pay half now, and the balance in six months?

EARNSHAW. How much is it for the year?

ME. $412.

EARNSHAW (*as he handed me his check with a satisfied expression on his face*). Well, I never dreamed that some day I would own *$100,000 of life insurance!*

ME. (*I must have looked at least as happy as he did. In fact, I was thrilled, and didn't try to hide it as I shook his hand.*) How long are you going to be here, Mr. Earnshaw?

EARNSHAW. I'll be going to lunch about 12:30. (*Looking at his watch, it was then about eleven o'clock.*)

ME. You look as though you never felt better in your life. May I have our doctor come over and see you, say about twelve o'clock?

EARNSHAW (*looking surprised*). Do I have to see another doctor?

ME. All the companies like to use their own doctors, Mr. Earnshaw. But since you just passed for the Travelers, our doctor won't be here long, I promise you. Is that all right?

EARNSHAW (*rather reluctantly*). Well . . . you better get him here before twelve o'clock.

I could hardly wait till I got down out of that building. The Travelers man had two days' start on me, and I realized that if he got to Mr. Earnshaw before I did, *anything* could happen! I nearly knocked a man over as I rushed out of the elevator to a pay-station phone.

Well, I got remarkably fast co-operation from the doctor, from everybody. Three days later, when I walked in and handed Mr. Earnshaw his policy, he said: "Boy! . . . you sure work fast! You beat the Travelers man back. He just phoned and said he's got my policy. He'll be over here with it later this morning."

The next day, Karl Collings said to me: "Say, did you insure a man by the name of Earnshaw?"

"Yes," I answered, surprised. "Why?"

"I met Elisha Oakford of the Travelers at lunch today. He said, 'Karl, do you have a man over there named Bettger?' 'Yes,' I said. 'Well, you tell the scoundrel I'm going to shoot him on sight!'

"Then," said Karl, "he told me he had insured Earnshaw for $25,000—had the Travelers issue an *extra* $25,000. After he delivered the first $25,000, Oakford said: 'Mr. Earnshaw, on the strength of the splendid examination you passed, I had an extra $25,000 issued. Here it is. You are under no obligation to take it, of course.'

"Earnshaw said, 'I'm sorry, another fellow beat you to it. He was the fastest worker I ever saw. He came in here two days *after* you—and was back with the policy two hours *before* you!' "

MAGIC PHRASE

"Good. You know something? You'll never be satisfied until you get it up to $100,000."

Emerson said, "One of the greatest services one man can render another, is to help him help himself." I believe one of the most important services a salesman can render is to help men *raise their sights!*

18.

A GOOD FRIEND of mine, one of the largest life insurance salesmen in Philadelphia, phoned me recently, saying that his company had issued a $100,000 policy with a "D" rating on an applicant of his, and the man refused to take it. He said: "Frank, I've heard that you have a special way of delivering substandard contracts. Would you be willing to go with me and try to sell this one?"

I said, "Joe, you flatter me. I didn't know I had any special way of delivering rated contracts, but if you think I might help in this case, I'll be glad to try."

Well, Joe made the appointment and we went out together to see the man.

Joe introduced me and gave me a nice buildup. Then the man waited for me to talk, but I waited for him. Soon, he started. I find prospects like it that way.

He was a husky, athletic looking fellow, and it was obvious that his pride had been hurt. He said he'd never had any trouble buying all the insurance he wanted at the regular rates, and he was going back to the company where he carried most of his insurance and he wouldn't have any trouble.

I listened attentively until he was completely through, then I said: "Mr. Doe, you've been a very successful businessman. Possibly you've had occasion to borrow money from your bank at times. Let's assume for a moment that you should go to your bank now and apply for another loan. A few days later your banker says to you: 'Mr. Doe, we have examined the statement you gave us and we find that there have been some changes in your company's assets—comparing them with your previous statement. However, we believe you should be able to improve this situation, so we've approved your loan for $100,000 at ___ per cent interest. When you are able to improve your balance sheet, we'll gladly reduce your interest rate. Is that satisfactory, Mr. Doe?'

"If your bank did make you such an offer, you wouldn't refuse the loan, would you?"

"I would, if I believed our statement justified a lower rate of interest. I'd go to another bank in a minute if I thought I could get a better rate."

"All right. That's fair enough," I agreed. "Let's look at the facts." Then I handed him the printed tables showing the pooled records of the leading companies. Mr. Doe was forty-one pounds overweight. The *actual* mortality rate at his weight and age was 45 per cent higher than average.

He examined the tables with genuine interest, then said: "I can get my weight back to normal within three or four months, and I'm going to do it."

"Good!" I said sincerely. "In the meantime, let's get this insurance in force right now. Let's put *you* in the driver's seat instead of the insurance company. If you can get your weight down in a natural way, you can clear this rating, and, in addition to that, you'll live longer. If your weight doesn't come down, or if any other condition should develop, you've got a contract that cannot be cancelled and the rate can never be increased!"

"No! . . . I don't want a rated policy!" he declared firmly. "I'm going to get my weight down and then I'll buy insurance at the standard rate."

"Mr. Doe, our job is to help you arrive at a practical decision. Suppose your company had just erected a new factory and the fire underwriters found certain fire hazards in your new building which made it necessary for them to charge an extra premium. You wouldn't refuse to insure the building while you were trying to remove the extra fire hazards, would you?"

"If I once pay this extra premium, the insurance company will never remove it!" he declared.

"Let's look at the facts," I urged. "The actual records prove that within ten years from the date of issue, one of three things has happened to every ten people having rated contracts: Four had the rating removed. Five became completely uninsurable. One died. Insurance companies are always happy to remove a rating. It's not *their* money, you know. They are merely trustees for hundreds of thousands of policyholders. So the removal of the rating really depends on *you*."

"Leave the policy with me a few days, and I'll let you know what I'm going to do." Picking up the contract, he looked at the premium again.

"Mr. Doe, we are in a position to do something for you right now that no other living person can do for you," I said in dead earnest.

"What's that?" he asked curiously.

"Insure your life for $100,000! Why don't you give us your check right now, and make this insurance effective?"

"This premium is too high. It's too much money!"

I paused a few moments, then said: "In addition to that, isn't there something else in the back of your mind that makes you hesitate to give us your check?"

"No, I just think this premium is too high, and I'm not going to pay it!"

"Mr. Doe, if you were my own brother, I'd say to you what I'm going to say to you now."

"What's that?" he asked.

"This extra premium will be one of the best investments you ever made, because I think you are going to do something about your weight and take the extra strain off your heart. Write your check now, and let's get started!"

Mr. Doe opened the policy and began glancing through it. There was absolute silence as he read. Joe and I exchanged a glance, but not a word was spoken. Finally, our man pulled a large checkbook out of his desk and asked: "Whom do I make this check payable to?"

As he handed the check to Joe, we both stood up and thanked him for his confidence. Then I said: "Mr. Doe, would you mind if I make one other suggestion?"

"No, go right ahead," said he, real pleasantly.

"Go to your own doctor and tell him what has happened, and follow his instructions in reducing your weight. I've found that insurance companies like it that way. Joe will follow up later in the year to see whether we can have your rating reduced."

After Joe and I walked down the street and got into his car he said: "So *that's* the way you deliver them!" "What do you mean?" I asked. "I thought you were licked—right down to the finish. I heard the guy say: 'The premium is too high *and I'm not going to pay it!*' Then the *next* thing I hear him say: 'Whom do I make this check payable to?' Honestly, Frank, I expected you to quit in the middle of that interview. That's what *I* would have done. That's why *I* failed to deliver that policy," Joe admitted.

"Joe," I said, "your record proves that you don't need anyone to tell you how to sell, but I've learned time and again that *you never know how close a man is to buying, by what he tells you.*"

Probably due to the fact that much of my selling has been to men above the average age, I have had a higher than average percentage of rated cases. In delivering them, I've found that a simple, straightforward story is best. If I have been able to do a pretty good information-getting job, I can usually anticipate the possibility of some rating, and prepare the prospect for it. Then I have less difficulty delivering the contract. In the event the contract is issued standard, it is often easy to deliver additional insurance.

In the case of "Mr. Doe," my friend Joe had done an excellent job of selling the need, but, because of the man's unusual athletic build, misjudged his weight.

Joe admitted that he always got panicky when he received a policy not issued as applied for. I reassured him that insurance companies are now able to classify risks with far greater accuracy, thanks to the extensive study and analysis of pooled information from the records of the principal companies. Knowing such a system exists, I feel that we can go out now and deliver rated contracts with complete confidence that the extra premium is a fair and proper charge.

Let me say, I have paid over three and a half million dollars of death and disability claims to date, and I have *never* had one widow, or any beneficiary, ask me how much the insured paid in premiums. In *every single instance,* the money was badly needed. In some instances, *desperately* needed. So, when I deliver a contract, standard or substandard, I believe it is impossible for me to be too enthusiastic about the service we are rendering.

Probably the best thing I ever did to help me deliver rated policies was to build a file marked "Substandard." It is surprising how quickly I can forget. So, whenever I hear anything that will help me, I put it in that folder. Then, the next time I receive a policy not issued as applied for, I pull out the folder and reread all the material and make notes on a 3 x 5 card of the ideas that seem to fit that case. Here again, I have found stories, appropriate stories, to be most effective to close the sale.

Oh, yes, don't forget that substandard policyholders have proven to be the best centers of influence! They better appreciate the advantages of "loading up" at standard rates, and lower rates at a younger age!

MAGIC PHRASES

". . . so, we've approved your loan for $100,000 at ____ per cent interest. If you are able to improve your balance sheet, we'll gladly reduce your rate of interest. Is that satisfactory, Mr. Doe? If your bank did make you such an offer, you wouldn't refuse the loan, would you?"

"All right. That's fair enough. Let's look at the facts." (Produce actual records.)

"Good! In the meantime, let's put YOU *in the driver's seat, instead of the insurance company."*

"Mr. Doe, our job is to help you arrive at a practical decision."

"Mr. Doe, if you were my own brother, I'd say to you what I'm going to say to you now."

A powerful confidence-gainer, if you can use it with absolute sincerity. But, if you can't, it's a hundred to one it will fail. And it *deserves* to fail!

19.

*How I Handle the Sale
When One or More Partners
Are Rejected*

ONE TIME I was referred to Charles R. Wolf, president of Miller, Bain, Beyer Company, one of the oldest and finest wholesale and retail dry goods firms in the city. Mr. Wolf was seventy years old, and his partners were sixty-seven, sixty-four, and forty-eight—all active in the business.

I was fortunate to be able to get all four of them together for an interview. In a few minutes, I sensed that someone previously had sold them on the idea of a "Buy-and-Sell Agreement," using life insurance to fund the agreement. But they had never gone through with the idea because, as they said, "the cost at our ages would make the plan prohibitive."

I said, "How do you know? Let's find out how much it *will* cost. Let the insurance companies make an offer. It won't cost you anything to find out. What have you got to lose?"

I waited, but nobody said anything, so I asked another question: "How long has it been since you were examined for life insurance?"

It had been a long while. Even the forty-eight-year-old man said he hadn't been examined for several years.

"Well," I said, "you are going to find it very interesting to see what kind of an examination you can pass now. You know an insurance examination is different from any examination by your own doctor. When will be the best time for our doctor to come down?"

Then, looking directly at the president, I asked: "What would be the best time for you, Mr. Wolf? Is morning better— or afternoon?"

"Morning would be better for me," he replied.

"Fine. Will tomorrow morning be all right—say about ten or ten-thirty?"

"That will be all right for me," agreed the president.

"How about your other men?" (Looking from one to the other) "Will you all be here tomorrow?"

They all seemed to think they'd be in the office pretty nearly all day, so I said, "Fine! After the doctor gets through with Mr. Wolf, he can take each one of you on at your convenience."

. . . Now let me say this frankly: I never had the slightest hope that all four of these men would pass the physical. And even if they did, I knew it would be impossible for them to pay the high cost at those ages. Besides, Mr. Wolf told me in the beginning that business was poor, and they were having trouble borrowing as much money as they needed from their bank. . . .

So I wasn't shocked when three out of the four were rejected. A contract was issued on the forty-eight-year-old man, William F. Allen, in the amount applied for.

I telephoned Mr. Wolf and made an appointment. When I told him I had been able to get only one contract issued, he wasn't surprised. I let him talk awhile, then handed the one contract to him and said, "Mr. Wolf, do you want to give me a check for Mr. Allen's policy?"

Now he *did* look surprised!

"No," he said firmly, "we wouldn't take this. If all of us had passed, and we could afford it, we would have gone ahead with the whole plan, but there is no point to it now."

"Now look," I said, with suppressed excitement, "let's suppose, just for a moment, that your company owned four buildings. Suppose the insurance companies refused to insure three of those four buildings. Would you refuse to take insurance on the one building on which they *did* issue a policy?"

"What's the point in taking this on Mr. Allen? He only owns one-quarter interest in the business," Mr. Wolf said.

"Isn't Mr. Allen a valuable man around here?"

"Yes, of course. He is a good man," admitted Mr. Wolf.

"Didn't you tell me that Mr. Allen is one of the best dry-goods men in the business?"

"Sure. There's none better," declared the president.

"He is a great deal younger than the other partners," I continued. "Didn't you say he is the spark plug around here now?"

"Yes, that is true," he agreed.

"You said you were having trouble getting as much credit at your bank as you need. Isn't it possible that if anything happened to Mr. Allen, his loss might seriously impair your credit?"

"No doubt about that, but really, Mr. Bettger, we can't afford to take on this additional expense right now," he said earnestly.

"Mr. Wolf, this insurance isn't going to cost you a dollar!" I declared.

"How do you mean?"

"Give me your check right now for $1,679. That pays the premium for a full year. Take this policy over to your bank tomorrow. Lay it down in front of your banker and say: 'We have been thinking about this for a long while. We realize it would be impossible for us to replace Mr. Allen if anything happened to him. He is probably the best dry-goods man in the business! We want to assign this insurance to you so that, if anything *should* happen to him, you will be safe with the money we owe you.'

"Mr. Wolf, this policy is going to help you solve one of your biggest problems . . . it will increase your credit at the bank. With the increased amount of money you can borrow, you can *far more* than pay the premiums on this insurance! And don't forget, if anything *should* happen to Mr. Allen, your loan at the bank would be wiped out, and you older men would be in a position to carry on—or, if you wanted to—sell out, and retire. *And it hasn't cost you a dollar!*"

Mr. Wolf gave me a check that day for the entire year's premium.

When they called Mr. Allen into the office and told him what they had done, his face lighted up and he seemed to be fighting back the tears.

The insurance this company bought that day on the life of this important key man actually *did* increase its credit, so the policy more than paid its way. It awakened both the bank and the members of the firm to a truer appreciation of William Allen's ability. Moreover, it let Mr. Allen know how much he was appreciated by everybody. He was inspired to become even more valuable than before. In fact, he virtually became president and Mr. Wolf acted more like "chairman of the board."

Shortly after I delivered that contract, I stopped in one day to see Mr. Wolf. I was really flattered by the warm reception he gave me. He couldn't have been more cordial had I been an old friend.

After chatting a few minutes, here is the interview that followed:

ME. Mr. Wolf, do you have any life insurance personally?

WOLF. (*He looked a little surprised at the question.*) Now you know I can't get insurance!

ME. No, I mean do you have any old policies? Insurance that you bought years ago?

WOLF. Oh, sure. I have some policies in the Travelers that I bought when I was a young man. They're all paid up now.

ME. May I see them?

WOLF. (*I thought he looked a little worried as he hastened to say:*) I wouldn't want to disturb those policies now. My wife isn't at all well. In fact, she requires a nurse constantly. I only have a day nurse for her, and I act as night nurse myself. If I should happen to go first, she will need that insurance money badly. (*He spoke with great feeling.*)

ME. I'm awfully sorry, Mr. Wolf. That must be a tremendous strain on you. How long has Mrs. Wolf been ill?

WOLF. She's been bedridden for thirteen years. She'll never be able to walk again . . . but the doctors say she will probably outlive me.

Further questions developed these facts: They had no children; his wife was the only one dependent on him, and she was two years older than he.

ME. Mr. Wolf, I believe I've got good news for you. I'm going to make a statement to you now that will sound *fantastic!* . . . Would you be surprised to discover that you can begin drawing an income immediately from the Travelers Insurance Company for all the rest of your life? . . . and then, at your death, if Mrs. Wolf survives you, she will continue to receive that same income every month for all the rest of her life?

WOLF. Why, that sounds impossible. I thought my insurance would only pay off at my death.

ME. May I see the policies?

WOLF. (*He opened the company's safe, found the policies in a private box of his own, and handed them to me. There were three, all Twenty Payment Life, taken out when he was in his thirties. He was now seventy. The cash values were very substantial.*)

ME. May I dictate a letter to your secretary, to go to the Travelers Insurance Company?

Mr. Wolf looked skeptical as he instructed his secretary to take down my letter. The letter merely asked for figures to convert the policies in the Travelers to a Joint and Survivorship Annuity for Mr. Wolf and his wife, giving the dates of birth of each.

He signed the letter. I told him that when he received a reply, if he would give me a call, I'd like to look it over before he signed anything.

Several days later, he phoned my office and left word that he had received the reply and he'd greatly appreciate it if I would come down as soon as possible.

It seemed like a "believe-it-or-not" deal! Because of the advanced ages of the insured and beneficiary, the Travelers agreed to pay an annuity beginning *immediately,* continuing every month thereafter as long as either of them lived; a sum greater than the amount stated on the original policies which would not start until *after* the death of the insured!

Naturally, Mr. Wolf was astonished by the whole transaction. "Now, there's one thing I want to know," he said finally. "Do the Travelers pay you a commission for this service?"

"No," I laughed, "of course not."

"Well, then, where do you get off in this deal?" he asked.

"Mr. Wolf, the tremendous satisfaction I get out of seeing you receive something you are entitled to, is worth *more to me* than any money you or any insurance company could pay me for such a service."

. . . Well, he lived many more years and never got over his amazement of how I had uncovered these "hidden benefits" which he received every month during the rest of his life. Benefits that might have remained dormant all those years and then finally gone to someone he probably never saw—because Mr. Wolf outlived his wife after all.

MAGIC PHRASE

"Now look, let's suppose, just for a moment, that your company owned four buildings. Suppose the insurance companies refused to insure three out of the four buildings. Would you refuse to take insurance on the one building on which they did issue a policy?"

20.

One of the Best Closing Tools
I Have in My Kit

I WAS GIVEN a name one time—"Smith & Jones," we'll call it—a firm of substantial heating contractors. A partnership. They had just been given the contract for heating a large new building to be constructed by the general contractors who gave me the lead. This should be a good time to see them.

I saw at a glance that one of the partners was definitely uninsurable. He weighed about ten pounds less than a horse and looked as if he must have a terrific blood pressure. But I went right ahead with the sale.

They agreed to be examined, and of course the big fellow was rejected. At that time, I couldn't even get a retirement annuity for him.

However, I had contracts issued on the other partner in the amount *fully* covering "Additional Capital Needed to Meet His Requirements."

When I went back and broke the news as gently as possible about the one partner being rejected, Mr. Smith said, "No, now look, we were interested in a partnership deal the way you presented it . . . that's *that!* I have all the personal insurance I want, but I was willing to go ahead if you could get us *both* through."

As he talked, his partner walked out of the room.

I pulled my chair up directly in front of Mr. Smith and looked him straight in the face. My voice was emotional as I said with deep feeling:

"Mr. Smith, you are in the heating business. You are doing business with architects and owners. Do I understand that when you are awarded a contract, as you have been recently, that you sign an agreement guaranteeing the plant you install will heat the building to 70 degrees in zero weather—is that right?"

SMITH. Yes, that's right.

ME. What *good* is your guarantee?

SMITH. Well, we have to put up a bond.

ME. You do? What does the bond mean?

SMITH. The bonding company guarantees that if our plant fails to heat to 70 degrees in zero weather, and I can't make it heat 70 degrees, another heating engineer would be called in; and the bonding company pays the extra charges.

ME. The bonding company makes good for *you*, is that right?

SMITH. Yes.

ME. Did you ever have any trouble getting one to heat 70 degrees in zero weather?

SMITH. No, we install a boiler 150 per cent over the requirement, and, of course, we can always raise that to greater than 70 degrees.

ME. Well listen . . . you have a wife and children . . . what if *something happens to you tonight? . . . your* home is heated . . . that is the zero hour for *you!* . . . right?

SMITH. That's right.

ME. *30 degrees!* Those are your own figures, not mine (*pointing to Balance Sheet*), 30 degrees for your family . . . *two degrees below freezing!*

That heating contractor bought an astonishing amount of insurance that day and gave me his check. We walked down the hall. He stopped at the door of his partner's office, put his arm around my shoulders and as the two of us leaned through the open doorway he told his partner what he had done—bought $100,000 of insurance. The partner looked at him in amazement and said: "How are you going to keep up all that insurance?"

"Listen," exclaimed Smith, *"I am heating my house to 70 degrees in zero weather!"*

After I realized the magic of this phrase, I made up my mind to go around to every heating contractor in Philadelphia and sell them *"70 degrees in zero weather!"* And I did sell a lot of them. Then one day it struck me: "Here! Every man I talk to has a home to heat . . . how about *him?* . . . you are taking an X-ray picture of his situation. And many of them are *30 degrees and under!"*

"70 degrees in zero weather" is one of the best "closing tools" I have in my *kit!*

. . . When I was a boy, digging ditches as a steamfitter's helper, it never occurred to me that one of the ideas I learned then would be helping me some day to keep the homefires burning.

I never got out of the heating business after all!

SUMMARY

PART THREE

1. The most important secret of salesmanship is to find out what the other fellow wants, then help him find the best way to get it.
2. There is only one way I've ever found to get anybody to do anything. And that is by making him *want* to do it.
3. It has been my experience that when you show a man what he wants, he will move heaven and earth to get it.
4. This universal law is of such paramount importance, it takes precedence over all other laws of human relations. It always has been, and always will be the most important. Yes, it looms up every day as Rule Number One over all other rules of civilization!

Little Things That Made Me a Better Salesman—No. 3

AFTER I DID THIS
I BEGAN TO SELL AS I NEVER SOLD BEFORE!

When I first started in the business, there was a man in our agency named Floyd Brown. I always wondered why Floyd didn't produce more business. He made a good appearance, talked well, had a lot of friends, and plenty of poise and self-confidence. I used to envy his ability to stand up at our agency meetings and express his ideas with such ease and complete lack of fear and nervousness.

Suddenly, Floyd took sick and died in four days. They said it was "walking typhoid"! He was only thirty-seven years old.

A few of us younger men in the agency served as pallbearers. After the services, we returned to his home to express our sympathy the best we could to his widow. The whole situation was tragic. We discovered that Floyd Brown had carried only $4,000 of life insurance—borrowed up to the limit.

Just a few months later, an older man in our agency died. He had been selling life insurance for thirty years. He likewise had all the earmarks of a big producer, yet always finished the year with about $150,-000. His death brought out the fact that he left only $5,000 of insurance.

To me, that seemed significant. I spoke to two men in the office about it. At that time, these two men were producing more business between them than all the other twenty-one in the agency put together!

They both said substantially the same thing: *"A man can't sell something he doesn't believe in himself.* How can you fight the most common objection of all, 'I can't afford it,' when it's so real to yourself?"

I asked big producers of other companies whom I

met at the Underwriters' meetings. Without exception, every one of them told me enthusiastically about *his own* big personal insurance program.

I asked them if they had built up this program *after* their income justified it and they said, No, they loaded up first and then worked like hell to pay for it!

At the time, I was having trouble meeting the premiums on $11,000 of Ordinary Life.

Suddenly an exciting idea hit me! I acted on it immediately. I filled in an application for $25,000 Ordinary Life and signed it myself! It seemed fantastic! My head actually swam as I wrote my name on the dotted line.

When I handed it to Jim Connor, then our cashier, Jim began to laugh it off. He thought I was just trying to be funny. When he saw that I was serious, he said, "Frank, how are you going to pay for it?"

"Go out and work like hell!" I declared. "It means increasing my production by $50,000, *only* $1,000 more a week!"

"Well," laughed Jim, as he caught the spirit of the idea, "I'm all for it myself. Sounds like a wonderful idea. But you'll have to *sell* the idea to the underwriting department. Your present income doesn't qualify your carrying $36,000!"

My enthusiasm sold the idea to our underwriting department. I started off paying monthly. They said they were going to watch me closely. They were afraid this was all a sudden rush of blood to my head and, when it came back to normal, I might wish I had given the scheme more sober thought.

. . . Well, I still have that $25,000. I have a real affection for that old policy. Later, I found myself doing the same thing on a bigger scale regularly.

What happened? Did I increase my production that extra $50,000? Listen, I jumped from 92nd to 13th in the entire company that year. At the next annual convention, I was called to the platform along with the other fifteen top producers of the Leaders' Club and presented with the usual award.

There has never been any doubt in my mind about it. I know the application I signed that day for $25,000 was my "Declaration of Independence" for myself and my family. It was my written pledge to self-organization. I *had* to do it! I had placed myself on the spot with my company . . . and *myself!*

I no longer feared that "King" of all objections, *"I can't afford it."* Instead of knocking me out in the first round, I was able to look my prospect straight in the eye with confidence and sincerity. The once famous "knockout punch" had lost its power! It was now an opportunity to close the sale; to help the other person raise his sights and become a really bigger and more substantial man.

I knew what it had done for me. I knew it would do the same for *anybody*. Now I could get myself warmed up to a real lather and spirit that *couldn't be licked!*

I began to sell as I never sold before!

PART FOUR

The World's Greatest Closer
of Sales!

21.

*The One Big Secret
of Closing Sales I Learned
from a Master Salesman*

I HAPPENED TO BE in New York recently, and walked smack into my old friend Richard Powell, at 42nd and Madison Avenue. Dick is a large personal producer in Philadelphia for the Manufacturers Life Insurance Company. He introduced me to a promising looking young man who is presently under his guidance.

Dick then turned to the young fellow and said: "Years ago, Jim, after my old supervisor, John Oliver, had taught me all he knew about the business, he suggested that I take Frank Bettger, a million dollar producer, to see some of my prospects, and *learn how he does it.*

"Two things amazed me," said Dick. "How quickly Frank gained the confidence and friendship of these strangers, and the amount of time he took to tell stories."

Laughingly, Dick turned to me and said: "Frank, I kept wondering when you were going to stop telling stories and start selling—and all the time the sale was being made and I didn't know it!"

I laughed and said: "Dick, I'm glad you brought that up. Years ago, when I first acted as 'bird dog' for Clayton Hunsicker, the greatest salesman I ever saw in action, I wondered the same thing, 'when will he stop telling stories and start selling!' I asked him about this one day, and here is what Clayt said:

" 'Frank, the World's Greatest Closer of Sales is ... STORIES!' "

I didn't go into any detail with Dick and his young protégé, because I knew Dick was capable of taking good care of that himself.

A few days later, I received a letter from Dick. Let me quote the last few lines:

> . . . your method of selling with stories was a revelation to me. There was not the slightest degree of tension or pressure on your part. I immediately adopted this procedure in all future interviews and it has paid me big dividends over the years. Frank, I want you to know that you gave me *the most valuable tool in my sales kit.*
>
> Gratefully yours,
>
> (Signed) DICK
>
> T. R. Powell

The motivating power of stories has been such a vital factor in whatever success I have had, that I am devoting this entire section to stories. In fact, throughout the book are stories I have told hundreds of times because I found them magic in helping me close sales. *They are not fictional.* Every one of them is an actual experience you may feel free to use.

I am not referring to the type of stories and jokes told by salesmen for entertainment purposes only. I don't condemn this practice. I know many successful salesmen who have a special gift for telling tall tales and no doubt it may help them sell themselves. But they know it doesn't sell their product. They soon get around to the *true* stories, *actual* experiences and examples where their product or services have helped people better their way of living; given them more security, helped businessmen increase their profits, decrease their losses, attract new customers, etc.

I was conducting a sales clinic not long ago in Kansas City, Missouri. A discouraged salesman came up to me one evening after I had talked on this subject. He said, "Mr. Bettger, people won't listen to my story." I said, "Tell me your story."

I listened and found what he thought was a story was not a story at all. He was just talking about his product.

I said, "Joe, I'm not interested in your story. I've got problems! If you've got something that is going to help me solve one of them—give it to me! . . ."

Shortly after I arrived home I received an exciting letter from Joe. His company had given him some wonderful action stories, dramatizing how their product was saving large factories and plants thousands of dollars in wasted man-hours. Direct testimonials from enthusiastic users.

Joe said: "Your magic phrases are really *magic*. I say: *'Would you be interested in an idea that will save your company thousands of dollars?'* They answer, 'Naturally.' I say: *'Good! I can tell you best by telling you a story.'*

"Then they listen eagerly and *want* to hear my story instead of getting rid of me in the first thirty seconds."

22.

A Powerful, Motivating Story

O NE HOT AUGUST morning, just as I was ready to leave the office, my phone rang. The message I received completely changed my plans for that day. It was the cashier's department: "We have two checks for one of your policyholders, John Scott. Do you want to deliver them, or shall we just mail them to him?"

"What are the checks for?" I asked.

"His retirement income contract has matured!" I heard.

"Do I want to deliver them?! Hold them right there," I yelled into the phone, "I'll be down in twenty seconds!"

It didn't seem possible that seven years had passed since I'd first walked into John Scott's office. All the excitement of that great event raced through my mind as I phoned Mr. Scott's office . . . for the "John Scott case" was the sale where I blindly stumbled onto *the most profound secret of successful selling!*

Imagine my disappointment when his secretary told me Mr. Scott was in Ocean City, N. J., and wouldn't be back for another month. She gave me his address.

Two hours later, I drove up in front of John Scott's summer cottage on Wesley Avenue in Ocean City. Mrs. Scott answered my ring at the front door. I had met her a few times previously. "Come right in, Mr. Bettger," she smiled. "Mr. Scott is on the porch upstairs taking a sun bath."

I found Mr. Scott enjoying a big porch rocker, facing the ocean. It was a glorious day! Not a cloud in the sky. He seemed pleasantly surprised as I approached him.

SCOTT. Why, how do you do, Mr. Bettger. What are you doing down around here?

ME. I've come all the way down from Philadelphia just to see you. I have brought good news to you!

SCOTT. What is it?

ME (*handing him a check for $416.67*). I could have mailed this to you, but I wanted to have the pleasure of handing it to you in person . . . *your first monthly income check!* And Mr. Scott, I'm going to say the same thing now that I said to you when I delivered your annuity contract seven years ago!

SCOTT. What's that?

ME. It's not enough. It ought to be *twice* as much!

SCOTT. Well, Mr. Bettger, I could just as well have made it twice as much, and I'm sorry now that I didn't, because I made some bad investments during the last few years. In fact (*looking around to make certain Mrs. Scott wasn't there*), I must tell you frankly, this annuity now looms up as a very important thing for me.

ME. I'm sure glad you've got it, Mr. Scott. And on the third of next month your mailman will deliver to you another check for $416.67, and every month thereafter for the rest of your life. Isn't that a comforting thought?

SCOTT. It certainly is.

ME. That is probably the reason why people who own annuities outlive the average person by several years. This annuity should help you live longer. Now, Mr. Scott, I have another surprise for you (*handing him another check*).

SCOTT. What is this?

ME. That is your dividend check for $1,222.

SCOTT. I don't understand. You mean this is something *extra?*

ME. Yes, sir. That's a dividend for good measure.

SCOTT. Well, that is perfectly amazing to me. In times like these, when so many people are breaking promises, your company does *more* than it guarantees. Another thing that surprises me, Mr. Bettger. I didn't expect to get this money until my seventieth birthday, and I'm not seventy until next December 24th.

ME. Mr. Scott, your policy reads, "On August 3rd, the Company agrees to pay John Scott, etc." That date is exactly seven years after the date we wrote your policy.

The Least Expected Happens Mostly!

John Scott lived and drew that income every month for six years. During those years, through a combination of circumstances, practically all his assets were swept away—except for his home. In fact, he became almost entirely dependent upon the income from his annuity.

He became ill, and I visited him once or twice at his home. Then one night, one of his sons called me on the phone and said: "Dad is desperately ill. Mother asked me to call you, Mr. Bettger. She says you are the only person living who could get Dad to change the beneficiary on his annuity. It is the *only* thing left now for Mother."

The next morning, I went up to Mr. Scott's home. They allowed me only five minutes with him. I was shocked when I saw him lying there in bed. He had failed so much I wouldn't have known him.

After a few moments of friendly conversation, here is what took place in as quiet and easy a manner as I could manage:

ME. Mr. Scott, a number of years ago when you bought your annuity you named certain Bible Schools as beneficiaries. At that time, your business was prospering and everything was fine. Since then, we have had a depression and many changes have taken place with everybody. Now I'm sure you are going to get well and everything will work out all right again. If it does, you can always name those schools again as beneficiaries. But in the meantime, if anything should happen to you, don't you think you should have this go to Mrs. Scott and your daughter Mary?

SCOTT. Well, Mr. Bettger, you know I took this insurance to protect those schools.

ME. Yes, I know you did, Mr. Scott, but right now, Mrs. Scott and Mary really need this protection. What is it the Bible says:

"He who provides not for his own, and especially for those of his own household, hath denied the Faith, and is worse than an infidel"?

SCOTT. *(With great difficulty, Mr. Scott raised up in bed on one elbow and with trembling hand signed the paper with my pen.) I've been worrying about this . . . but now I can forget it.*

Sixty days later, John Scott passed away. There was a substantial balance of principal which we arranged for Mrs. Scott, then seventy-six years old, to draw in monthly installments. She passed away two years later, and Mary, in turn, began receiving a modified monthly income which she is now getting and will continue to receive as long as she lives.

Since I first met John Scott, I have insured five of his sons; thirty-five of his employees; one nephew; a contractor who had done work for their company; also a hauling contractor; his doctor; his lawyer—a total of fifty-three different people for a total of $781,000 of life insurance. At one time their premiums amounted to $34,699 annually.

But important as this was, even more important was the motivating power of the John Scott story itself. I have told it countless times in closing sales.

I make it a point never to violate a confidence. I am always careful to say, before I begin this story, "Here is a story I can tell you, because it is an open secret on the street. You might call it *The Least Expected Happens Mostly.*

23.

The Felix Isman Story

IN PHILADELPHIA, many years ago, there lived one of the most fabulously successful real estate men in the world. His name was Felix Isman.

One day, Mr. Isman invested $100,000 in an annuity. At the time, he said, "I never expect to go broke. But I have seen so many men come into my office lately who have lost everything ... men who were just as smart and just as successful as I have ever been, that I've made up my mind to buy this annuity. Then if I ever should go broke, here is one thing that I can never lose. Creditors can't take it away from me. I can't even give it away!"

Well, only a few years after he bought that annuity, Felix Isman went broke. His creditors took everything. Everything that is, except his annuity! They even tried to attach that! But an annuity is nonattachable under Federal law.

Now all his life, Felix Isman possessed a great desire to write. If only he could get enough time, he believed he could write.

Here was his chance!

So instead of going back into the real estate business, he decided to move to New York and change his scale of living— so that he and his wife could live modestly in a small apartment on his income of only $5,700 a year from that annuity.

He had very little formal education. His friends thought it ridiculous for him to think he could write. But Felix Isman had some sort of gift for painting pictures with words. His writing was alive and colorful.

Magazines began accepting his stories.

The *Saturday Evening Post* sent him to Florida to write a story about the amazing Florida real estate boom which had caught the attention of the entire nation.

Felix Isman became so excited over the fantastic profits—people becoming "rich overnight"—that he flew back to New York and tried to "sell' his annuity back to the insurance company.

They told him it was against the law. They couldn't.

He offered to accept a settlement of fifty per cent. But the insurance company refused.

He threatened to sue them, and took it up with a New York lawyer.

The lawyer looked up the "law" and said the insurance company was right. "It would be illegal. . . ."

Felix Isman returned to Florida a bitterly disappointed man, because he saw an opportunity lost to make another fortune.

But only a few weeks after he returned to Florida, the boom *burst! The whole thing blew up right in front of him!*

. . . Felix Isman later wrote that he got down on his knees and thanked God that he had been saved from committing *financial suicide!*

I always save this story for the "close." I have told it hundreds of times, yet I always feel *real* emotion as I tell it; because it is so human and I know every word of it is true.

When the sale has reached the time for decision, this story is a *compulsory next step!*

The ball is now down on his "one-yard line." Momentum is with *you!* All you need now is a fountain pen!

24.

This Story Helps Me Get a Check with the Order

RECORDS OF SUCCESSFUL life insurance salesmen prove that most of them obtain some kind of settlement with the application. I have talked with million dollar producers all over the country and they have told me that asking for a check at the time the prospect signs the application is *one of the most powerful factors in closing the sale.*

The man then places a higher value and greater appreciation on our service. Once he pays something, even if it is only a small deposit, he feels that the product is his property. If it is insurance, usually he tells his wife, or someone, that he has "just *bought* more life insurance." Once he has paid some money, the matter is settled in his mind.

But if he pays *nothing,* he has time to review and debate alone, and frequently decides to postpone action.

I've never had a man cancel an order once he has paid me something on account!

I used to be *afraid* to ask for money, but after I tried it a few times, I lost that fear. As soon as a man finishes signing his name, I say in a natural, easy manner, "Do you want to give me a check for the full year, Mr. Harris, or would you rather just pay half now, and the balance in six months?"

Generally he says: "How much is it?" or "How much is it if I only pay half now?" Sometimes he asks if he may pay quarterly.

Now, when they balk at this point—there is the critical moment!

If he says, "Can't I pay for it after I see the policy?" or "I haven't entirely made up my mind about this, I thought we'd go ahead with the examination" or "If I pass, you can bring the policy to me so that I can look it over" ... *here's the story I've found so effective.*

I say, "Mr. Harris, I had a lesson taught me a number of years ago. Three partners agreed to let me have them examined for partnership insurance. All three passed and I took the policies to them. After going over the contracts with two of the men, I said, 'Where is your other partner, Mr. Curtis?'

"Both men laughed, and the older man said: 'That's a funny one. The day after your doctor was here, Charlie's wife phoned and said: "Charles won't be in today. He's got a terrible cold." And by golly, now he's a pretty sick man. He's got *pneumonia!*'

"I looked sick! I said, 'I'm awfully sorry you told me that.'

" 'Why?' asked one of them, looking surprised, 'does that make any difference with these policies?'

" 'I can't deliver this one on Mr. Curtis now,' I answered.

" 'When *can* you deliver it?' he asked, getting hot.

" 'We'll have to wait until Mr. Curtis has completely recovered, then later have him re-examined.'

" 'How long will that take?' the younger man asked.

" 'Possibly two or three months,' I admitted.

" 'Listen,' asked the older man, 'wasn't there some other way you could have handled it so that this couldn't have happened?'

" 'Yes,' I confessed, 'if you had given me a check for part of the premium at the time you all signed the applications, the insurance would automatically have gone into effect as soon as you were approved at the head office.'

" *'Well why didn't you ask us for a check?'*

" 'Because I wasn't sure whether you had completely made up your mind to buy the insurance, and I was afraid you might think I was trying to high-pressure you.'

" 'Well, I would call that damned lousy service, Mr. Bettger,' said the older man.

"I agreed with him and told them it was a lesson for me.

That I'd never fail again to try to get some kind of settlement with an application. And I never have!

"Well, they looked pretty disgusted, but finally gave me a check for their two contracts. I returned the other policy to the company with a letter explaining the situation. It took four months before that third partner was well enough to have a policy reissued on him and put in force. Since that experience, I seldom fail to get some kind of deposit with an application."

. . . I have found this story surprisingly effective. Usually, as I come down to the end, the prospect is no longer listening to me but is writing out a check!

MAGIC PHRASE

"Do you want to give me a check for the full year, Mr. Harris, or would you rather just pay half now, and the balance in six months?"

25.

*How to Make It Easy
for Young Husbands and Wives
to Buy*

HERE IS A SIMPLE little idea I picked up when I was
young in the business. The reason I liked it, frankly, was
because it simplified for *me* the various forms of policies and
helped me decide which was the best plan for me to buy *myself*.

So I began using it, and it has helped me close many sales
on people who were confused and couldn't decide what they
wanted.

For example: Just recently I was referred by a friend to a
young man, twenty-seven, married, with a four-month-old baby.
This man had *no* life insurance!

I phoned him at his office, and asked if I might see him and
his wife some evening at their home.

The following evening, as I sat down with them in their
attractive little living room, they waited for me to talk, but I
waited for them.

The husband began to talk, and I soon learned that insurance
men had been on his heels day and night. As I encouraged him
to talk, his wife soon joined in. They had gone through several
workouts with insurance men and now they seemed more confused than ever.

ME. How long have you been thinking about buying this
insurance?

HUSBAND. I guess we didn't really begin to think seriously about it until the baby was born.

ME. That's four months ago?

HUSBAND. Yes.

ME. And you haven't arrived at a decision yet. Is that right?

WIFE. We've just about made up our minds to buy $10,000 in the Blank Company. It's one of the cheapest policies we've found, and it's flexible. We can change it to anything else we want within the next five years. (*With that, she pulled out a stack of eight illustrations in various companies and handed me the one they thought they liked best.*)

ME (*I read it quickly*). This is an excellent plan. You have decided to take this one, have you?

HUSBAND (*hesitatingly*). . . . Well—uh—we told the agent we wanted another week to think it over.

ME. Have you been examined by their doctor?

HUSBAND. Oh, no! I haven't been examined.

ME. You are not sure yet, are you?

HUSBAND. No. (*they both admitted*).

ME. Well, that's *my* job to help you arrive at a final decision. In order to do this, let me give you a short course in life insurance that may make it easier for you to decide (*This I always say with a grin*).

I drew my chair in such a position that they both could see my drawings. (This is very elementary, but I find that people follow it with great interest): First, I put the prospect's age down on the left side of my paper, drew a straight line to the other side and wrote 100.

27 ———————————————— 100

Then I said, "The first policy ever written was called an 'Ordinary Life Policy.' Some companies call it 'Whole Life,' because you pay during your whole life. However, if you live to Age 100 (and I say this with a big grin) the insurance company will pay you the face amount of the policy, say $10,000. In the beginning, this was hard to sell. People hated to buy something where they had to 'die to win.' Salesmen couldn't make a decent living, so it was hard to keep them in the business.

"Later, the companies conceived the idea of charging more, so that your policy became paid in full in twenty years. It's the same contract, an endowment at 100, but the insured gets through paying in twenty years. (I always make this second drawing just under the first).

27 _____ 100
                    Twenty Payment Life

"Then, of course, came the ten, fifteen, twenty-five and thirty Payment Life.

"Later, salesmen said: 'If you could just give us a policy to sell where the man won't have to die to win. A plan that would pay *him* if he lives.' So the companies developed the 20 Year Endowment (third drawing).

                                                 47
27 _____
                                  20 Year Endowment

"And, of course, later—the ten, fifteen, twenty-five, thirty and even thirty-five Year Endowment. Naturally, the endowment form of policy is the highest priced plan.

"There is one other plan, called 'term insurance.' Term insurance is like fire insurance, it only pays if you die. It has no cash or loan value and may only be carried for a limited number of years—then it must be converted to one of the regular forms I've shown above.

"Every form of policy sold by life insurance companies is *basically* one of those four forms.

"Now here is an interesting fact, I think a very *significant* fact. After more than a hundred years, which of these plans do you suppose has always been, and continues even today to be, the biggest seller?" (Everybody eagerly wants to know the answer to this question.)

"*Eighty-one per cent*—81 per cent of the people buy the original plan, Ordinary Life!

"Why? Well, it gives you the greatest amount of protection

for the least amount of money. And it is the most *flexible* . . . because, at any time, you may stop paying and receive a paid-up policy in exact proportion to the amount of money you have paid. If at any time you've got more money than you need, and you want a safe place to invest it, you may convert your Ordinary Life Policy to twenty Payment, ten Payment, or an endowment to mature at any age you select. And you may do this without a medical re-examination! In other words, *you are in the driver's seat at all times, and you can do anything you want with an Ordinary Life policy."*

. . . I left them shortly afterward with their check for $10,000 Ordinary Life with Family Maintenance for 20 Years, and waiver of premium. In other words, after the little "short course" they quickly came to a decision for Ordinary Life. Then it was easy to explain to them how they could get the maximum protection they needed by adding Family Maintenance; and waiver of premium in the event of disability.

People do like to *understand* what they are buying. I've used this little thumbnail education of policy forms countless times, and I find that people, young and old, love it. Even men who have bought large amounts of insurance love it.

Before I left that young couple that night, I asked whether I might have a peep at that little baby. They were pleased by this and I really never saw a more beautiful child. They both came to the front door with me and seemed mighty happy about the whole thing as they waved "Good night."

26.

Bring On Your Witnesses

RECENTLY A LAWYER named Jorge Artel was defending an old farmer who had been brought to trial on a charge of murder. Artel was convinced that his client was innocent, but as he spoke to the jury, citing one complicated legal ruling after another, he could feel the attitude of the jurors change from respect to indifference and boredom.

Then he noticed that one policeman in the courtroom was not listening at all. He was stealing glances at a copy of the *Reader's Digest*.

"Suddenly," wrote Artel, "it occurred to me that I had read several stories in that magazine about men whose lives had been put in jeopardy by courtroom errors. *Why wouldn't these stories of actual, individual experiences* have a more positive effect on the jury than all my involved technical citations? Hastily, I requested an adjournment, which was granted.

"Next morning, I came to the court with three articles: 'Miracle of the Gallows'; 'Tillie Scrubbed On'; and 'That's the Man!'; all true stories that had appeared in the *Reader's Digest*. As I read these articles to the jurors, they looked into the troubled eyes of the old farmer. Almost miraculously, those three stories had done what legal quotations and formal arguments could not do. In a few moments, my client walked out of the courtroom a free man.

"My confidence in my client was vindicated two months later, when another man confessed to the crime."

Years ago, I had photostatic copies made of several testimonial letters. Coming down toward the close of the sale, I usually say: "Mr. Doerr, naturally I am prejudiced. Anything I say about this plan would be favorable" . . . then I produce two or three letters appropriate to his situation.

I think of this much the same as a trial lawyer bringing on his witnesses!

DALE CARNEGIE
27 WENDOVER ROAD
FOREST HILLS
NEW YORK CITY

November 11, 19—.

Mr. Frank Bettger
Fidelity Mutual Life Insurance Company
Philadelphia, Pennsylvania

My dear Frank Bettger:

I recently spent an hour going over all my life insurance policies. I bought my first policy from you on March 16, 1920. Do you know that as I look over that policy and the other policies I have bought from you since then, I ask myself "What would have become of this money if I had not put it in life insurance?" I would probably have very little of it today. It would probably have gone the same way that much of my savings did. I lost a great deal in the stock market and I also lent several thousand dollars to friends; and only a small percentage of these loans have ever been, or ever will be, returned. I also made other investments which not only resulted in financial loss but also in worries and headaches. But my life insurance has brought me no headaches, no losses.

As I looked over these policies, I said to myself

"How fortunate I was to put my money in this life insurance."

I wonder, Frank, if you ever met a man of fifty who was sorry he had put money in life insurance twenty or thirty years previously. Frankly, as I look back over my life, I wish a court had appointed you as my guardian (and I am not joking about this) on March 16, 1920, and that I had been forced to turn every dollar of my savings over to you, outside of what I invested in my home, for investment in annuities.

Back in 1920 when I was thirty-two, I thought I knew how to invest money and, of course, the generation coming on now entertains that same feeling.

After living fifty four years I have now come to the conclusion that it is almost as difficult to invest money wisely as it is to make it.

You are doing young men especially, Frank, a big favor when you put pressure on them to invest all their savings in insurance or annuities.

If you want to show this letter to anybody who is hesitating about buying insurance, you have my permission to do so.

The best of luck!

Sincerely,

(Dale Carnegie)

GEORGE E. CANTRELL
REAL ESTATE TRUST BUILDING
PHILADELPHIA, PENNA.

September 9, 19—.

Dear Frank:

Thank you for check and notation. I suppose Ed told you I am retiring from business. I expect to have everything cleaned up by October 15. This annuity is playing an important part in my retirement plan. My only regret is that I didn't take twice as much when I began buying this insurance from you years ago. Through unwise investments, I lost several times what this annuity cost me besides the care and worry.

If young men could only realize how much better off they'd be financially and mentally by saving their money through a good insurance company like the Fidelity.

Well, here's to you—you are one of the finest guys I ever met. Not because of the check but you were always that way.

And my best wishes and Good Health—Good Luck and everything else that is good in this old world of ours.

Next time we meet, you will do the pitching and I will catch.

Good luck again.

Sincerely,

George

I sit quietly while the prospect reads. Now my "witness" is telling *his own story*.

Frequently, I call one of my "witnesses" on the phone—preferably someone the prospect knows . . . a neighbor, friend, competitor. Sometimes, it's an out-of-town call. Long distance calls, I find most effective. (Now remember! I make this call on my prospect's phone. I ask the operator to report back the cost of the call, and I *always pay it immediately*.)

I found these "witnesses" exerted a powerful influence in establishing confidence for me among strangers.

. . . So an effective way to win a man's confidence and motivate him to *action* is to:

BRING ON YOUR WITNESSES

MAGIC PHRASES

"Mr. Doerr, naturally, I am prejudiced. Anything I say about this plan would be favorable" (then I produce two or three appropriate letters).

Bringing my "witness" on by telephone, I find much more effective than testimonial letters. For example, after I say, "Mr. Doerr, naturally, I am prejudiced," etc., I add, *"so I want you to talk with someone who has no interest in selling it. May I use your telephone for a minute?"*

Then I call one of my witnesses on the phone and let my prospect talk to him. I prefer it to be someone the prospect knows, or knows something about.

27.

The Profits from this Story Founded a Great University and Put Thousands of Young Men Through College

THE BEST PREACHERS I ever heard were all great salesmen. And every one of them did most of their selling with *stories!*

The greatest preacher I ever had the good fortune to hear, was *Russell Conwell.* He started his famous lecture, "Acres of Diamonds" right off with a wonderful story about an ancient Persian named Ali Hafed, who sold his prosperous farm; left his family; went away in search of a fabulous diamond mine in far-off places; and at last died in a foreign land, in rags, wretchedness, and complete poverty. He never knew that soon after his death, the richest diamond mines ever discovered—the mines of Golconda—were to be unearthed in his own back yard!

The famous "Acres of Diamonds" lecture given over six thousand times by Russell Conwell, the *founder* of Temple University, tells this story of Ali Hafed . . . and draws its obvious, but ever fresh moral. And the *start* of this great university was founded on the philosophy (and the financial returns!) of this lecture.

Through the years, thousands all over the country have found in their own back yard a mine greater than Golconda—a mine of knowledge and education leading them into the wealth of broadened and more successful lives. Temple University is today dedicated, as it has always been, to the purpose stated by its founder, Russell H. Conwell, "to make an education possible for all young men and young women who have good minds and the will to work."

Perhaps you could use some of Russell Conwell's stories to help sell *your* services. A copy of the famous "Acres of Diamonds," in an attractively printed edition, will be mailed to you gladly, without cost, if you write to Temple University, Philadelphia, Pa.

SUMMARY

PART FOUR

Selling, in a large sense, is story-telling, for you are telling the story about your "goods." Therefore, developing this art should constitute one of the most important studies of a salesman.

Of course, your story or example must relate directly to some problem of the prospect. I soon found, if you get off the beam and leave him or his problem out of the picture, he becomes nervous and bored and has no time to listen. He must be the central figure in the story. As long as he is, he is interested. Violently interested. *He sells himself!*

Why don't you cultivate the story-telling method used by that *great* salesmen whose thirty-five parables have lived through the centuries and are selling people just as successfully today as they did more than *nineteen hundred years ago?*

If you want to be more successful, if you want to *close more sales,* why don't *you* follow the example set nineteen hundred years ago by the greatest salesman who ever walked this earth? *Jesus.*

HOW "DADDY'S LITTLE GIRL" CLOSES
MANY SALES FOR ME

I was talking with a vice-president of the Corn Exchange Bank in Philadelphia one morning. His office was right out in the open, so that from his desk you can see all the way through the bank to the entrance.

Suddenly, he put his hand on my arm and interrupted me: "Wait a minute!" said he, looking out toward the teller's window. "If you want to hear a real life insurance story, just listen to this."

One of the cutest little girls I've ever seen, about five years old, was running ahead of her mother toward us. She stopped at the teller's window close to us. She was so small that her head hardly showed above the counter as she got up on her tiptoes and pushed a piece of paper through the caged window.

She seemed to know the teller and in a wee voice said, "Oh, Mr. Blake, here's another check from my Daddy!" The teller said, "That's just fine!" The mother arrived at the window now—she was rather a young woman—the teller cashed the check and pushed the money out through the window to them. The little girl thanked him very much and the mother thanked him, and together they walked out of the bank.

I said to the vice-president, "What is this?"

He said, "Here's the story. That young woman is a widow, and that's her little girl. They come in here every month and cash the check that comes to them from an insurance company. The little girl thinks her father is away on a long trip. Her mother hasn't told her yet that Daddy isn't coming back. Just about three months before the father's death, he took out a policy with Millard Orr of the Massachusetts Mutual. Do you know Millard?"

"Yes," I said, "I know him well."

"Well," he continued, "Millard sold this insurance to the man when he was apparently in perfectly good health. It provides $150 a month to his widow for twenty years, and at the end of twenty years, she'll receive a smaller income for all the rest of her life."

That little scene I witnessed left such a deep impression on me that every time I tell it when I'm trying to sell a man, I feel the same emotion I had that day in the bank.

Wouldn't Daddy be astonished if he knew how much life insurance "Daddy's Little Girl" has helped to sell?

PART FIVE

An Exciting New Field of Business That Put Me into the "Big Leagues"

28.

I Became a Bird Dog
for One of the Nation's
Greatest Salesmen

IN MY EARLY DAYS in the business, I had the good fortune to become associated with Clayton M. Hunsicker, the greatest salesman I ever saw in action. At that time, he was a man nearly twice my age. I want to tell you how it happened that a green, blundering dub like I was could team up with one of the truly greats.

I heard Mr. Hunsicker make a wonderful talk on business perpetuation before the Life Underwriters' Association at the Bellevue-Stratford Hotel in Philadelphia. I was tremendously impressed and realized then the great possibilities this new field of life underwriting opened up. But I also realized that I could never learn how to do it myself merely by listening to speeches.

So, after the meeting, I waited for this great salesman at the hotel entrance. Finally, he came out with several other men, and they started up Broad Street. I joined them somewhat like a kid would walk alongside of celebrities. When we came to the next corner, these men shook hands with Clayt and left him. I was scared, but I thought there was no harm in trying. When he continued up the street, I walked next to him and said: "Mr. Hunsicker, that was a wonderful talk you made today. It was the best I ever heard at an underwriters' meeting."

He looked pleased and smiled as he said, "Thank you."

Then I ventured this question: "Mr. Hunsicker, if I should

arrange some appointments for you with heads of business in the city, would you be willing to go out with me on them?"

To my surprise, he quickly replied, "Certainly!"

"If we should do some business together, how would we work out the commission?" I was a nobody and he was such a big man in the business, known throughout the country, that I was amazed when he said: "There's only one fair way to handle that—fifty-fifty."

Well, that was the beginning of a part-time partnership that lasted several years. If I can lay claim to anything I ever did that was smart, that was it. Other small producers could have worked with Clayt the same way that I did, but they didn't like the idea of splitting their commission. They would come to him for advice and ask him a lot of questions about cases they were working on, but that was all.

I always figured that half a loaf was better than none. In fact, when I first approached Hunsicker, if he had said the division of commissions would be 75%-25%, I would have gladly accepted the 25% and felt it was still a good deal for me while I was learning.

Generally speaking, I don't believe in joint work in selling . . . except where it is possible to get an outstanding producer to work with an inexperienced man, or a small producer, in somewhat the same relationship I had with Mr. Hunsicker. That's the way it is done in other professions. Great surgeons usually start as understudies to great surgeons.

I soon learned the secret of his success as a great closer. Clayt Hunsicker sold largely by telling stories! He was a marvelous story-teller.

I asked him about this one day. I said, "Mr. Hunsicker, I am amazed at the amount of time busy businessmen are willing to give you. They just sit there listening, and seem to forget all about time."

Hunsicker said, "The secret of *that* is that I always make sure my story *fits*. The story reveals a tragic situation that *could* happen to them. That's why they are anxious to hear the solution."

After I had been acting as "bird dog" for Hunsicker a couple of years, I telephoned a policyholder of mine, treasurer of a large manufacturing corporation. I told him I had something important I wanted to tell him; would he be able to see me for about fifteen minutes if I came right down?

He couldn't see me that day but agreed to see me the following morning.

Nine-thirty the next morning, I was in his office; he was a man sixty years of age. "What's on your mind, Mr. Bettger?" he asked.

I had formed the practice of opening up with one of Mr. Hunsicker's favorite stories. "Mr. Ellis," I began, "I can tell you best with a story. I am associated with a man named Clayton M. Hunsicker. Mr. Hunsicker has been in the life insurance business for thirty-eight years. A number of years ago, he went down to Ridley Park, Pennsylvania, and delivered a $25,000 check to the widow of one of his policyholders who had just died. As Mr. Hunsicker started to leave, he said:

" 'Mrs. Haines, I've never been able to sell your husband's brother, John. Do you think this would be a good time to try to sell him again?'

" 'I certainly do, Mr. Hunsicker,' she agreed. 'This has been almost as big a shock to John as it has been to me. He realizes now the importance of life insurance.'

"So, Mr. Hunsicker went right down to Chester, and interviewed the surviving brother.

"John said: 'Well, Mr. Hunsicker, I am going to buy some insurance, and I want you to handle it for me. You see, Tom and I owned fifty-two per cent of the stock in the business equally between us. So we had an agreement providing that if one of us died, the survivor would have the option of buying the deceased's interest at book value. This means that I will have to borrow from the bank, and I thought I'd take out enough insurance to protect the bank in the event of my death.'

"Mr. Hunsicker said: 'May I make a suggestion?'

" 'Certainly,' answered Mr. Haines, 'what is it?'

" 'How long has it been since you were examined for life insurance?'

" 'Frankly, I've never been examined for insurance. But I don't think I'll have any trouble passing,' Mr. Haines said.

" 'Then before you mention it to the bank, I'd suggest you let me have Dr. Van Dervoort look you over and get you approved for any amount you might decide on,' said Hunsicker. 'You see, if you tell the bank you are going to assign insurance to them, and later, tell them you can't get insurance, it might cause you some embarrassment, isn't that right?'

". . . Well, Mr. Hunsicker had Mr. Haines examined and approved. He had a policy issued for the amount Mr. Haines mentioned he might need. When he returned to Chester with the policy, confident that he had a big sale, Hunsicker had a shock coming to him.

"Mr. Haines said: 'Mr. Hunsicker, I'm not going to take that insurance!'

" 'Why not?' asked Hunsicker.

" 'What do you think that fool woman has done? I went up to Ridley Park and showed her the audit made by one of the largest accounting firms in Philadelphia. She said: "You will have to see my lawyer. I don't know anything about business, so I have turned the whole matter over to him."

" 'Why Ann, you don't have to do that,' said Haines. 'That will cost you a lot of money. I will handle this just the way I expected Tom to handle it for Mary, if I had gone first. Don't you trust me?'

" 'Mr. Hunsicker,' said Mr. Haines, 'I have been up there to see that fool woman *three times,* trying to reason with her. We had all been so friendly during my brother's lifetime. Now this . . .'

" 'And at a big cost to her,' he continued, 'her lawyer had another firm of accountants make an audit of our books, and they added a ridiculous amount for "Good Will." The price they set is nearly *double* what the business is worth! Do you know what I am going to do? I'm going to *quit!* I have enough money to live on in a modest way. So I've made up my mind to retire.'

"To make a very long story short, John Haines sold his interest in that business for a small price to 'Old Man Knabe' who founded the business, but who later went west and became wealthy in oil. Knabe sent his son on to manage the business, but the son didn't like it. Then they hired a manager, but the business rapidly went down hill and was finally liquidated. Tom Haines' widow never did get any dividends, and eventually received a few-cents-on-the-dollar settlement.

"That experience, Mr. Ellis, taught Hunsicker a lesson. Since that time, he has been helping businessmen arrange their affairs in such a way as to prevent anything like that from happening; an iron-clad agreement that protects everyone concerned: the widow, to make sure she receives a fair settlement; and the surviving partners, so that they are not harassed and worried in carrying on the business."

There was a long pause.

Suddenly, Mr. Ellis got up without a word and walked out of the room. I was afraid I had said something to offend him. But pretty soon he came back, followed by a very tall man. Mr. Ellis introduced me. He said, "Mr. Bettger, this is Mr. Houser, vice-president of our company. I would like him to hear what you have been telling me, because he and I have discussed our situation here and we've realized for some time that we should do something about it."

I repeated the Haines story just as I had told it to Mr. Ellis. Then I asked them some questions.

Here is the information they gave me: Four of the owners were running the business, all of them past fifty. Each had a wife and children. These four men—the president, vice-president, secretary, and treasurer—owned 10/15th of the stock, divided almost equally among them. The balance of the stock, 5/15th, was owned by widows and children, some of them minors, who had inherited the stock from former owners.

It was easy to point out the critical situation confronting them. Upon the death of any one of the four, *controlling* stock would pass into the hands of inactive women and children, the surviving three men being left to run the business with a *mi-*

nority interest! Thus they would lose control, with several in-experienced women and their lawyers—and other lawyers repre-senting minor children, telling them how to run the business! Regulating their salaries! Probably putting in an "efficiency expert" to dictate to them!

As I left, I knew I had made a good start toward a sale. They agreed to an appointment with Mr. Hunsicker and myself for the following Tuesday morning at eleven o'clock and promised to have all four officers present.

That afternoon, I told Mr. Hunsicker all about my inter-view. It sounded promising to him, and he agreed to go with me.

I checked with him again on Sunday, and he said he'd meet me on the first floor of the Drexel Building in Philadelphia, where this company had its offices.

Tuesday morning at 10:55 A.M. I was pacing back and forth from the elevators to the front entrance of the building, I was so excited. At 11:00 A.M. Hunsicker hadn't shown up. I phoned his office. His secretary was bewildered. "Mr. Hunsicker must have forgotten about your appointment, because only a few minutes ago he called me from a steel plant up in Consho-hocken."

What an awful blow! My first thought was to call Mr. Ellis and tell him that Mr. Hunsicker was ill and ask whether he could possibly make it for a later date. Then I thought, "No! I know this story backward and forward. Why should I be afraid? I'm going up there alone!

29.

*The Secret of How I Made
One of My Biggest Sales*

I WAS USHERED into Mr. Ellis' office. He called for the
other three officers of the company. They were distinguished
and important-looking men. After I was introduced, we all sat
down. I was nervous. I was scared. But I had made up my mind
to make this *the most enthusiastic interview I ever had!*

There were a few moments of silence. They looked at me,
and I looked at them. Mr. Phelps, the president, broke the
silence: "Mr. Ellis said you talked with him and Mr. Houser
about an idea, and he thought we should all get together and
give it some consideration."

I expected them to ask where Mr. Hunsicker was, and I was
prepared to explain—but they never did. So I acted as though
there was nothing strange about my appearing there all alone.

Now I had already told the Haines story twice, and I thought
Mr. Ellis might have repeated some of it to the others, so I
decided to start off with a story that none of them had heard:

Here's the way I began:

"I can save you time, and give you the idea best by telling
you a story . . . A few years ago, a neighbor of mine named
Armstrong died. He was one of three brothers who owned the
Armstrong Manufacturing Company. These brothers had an
agreement providing that in the event of the death of one, the
surviving brothers were to pay the widow of the deceased $80,000
under an absolute contract of sale, in payment of the deceased's
entire interest in the business. Half of the amount, $40,000, was

provided by life insurance, and the other half to be paid within sixty days after the death of the owner. Well, the widow thought the price was absolute robbery, that these two brothers were taking unfair advantage of her. 'Why,' she said, 'if my husband knew what you were doing, he would rise up out of his grave.' She hired a lawyer and took it to court. . . .

"I was there at that trial, ready to testify why and how the agreement had been entered into by all three brothers. But I was never called on. The late Judge Patterson of the Orphans' Court was on the bench. He stopped the lawyer representing the widow right in the middle of his plea and said:

" 'Just a minute . . . you haven't got a case here. You have no contest!'

"The lawyer looked at Judge Patterson, surprised: 'Your Honor, what do you mean, "we have no contest"? Anything can be contested, can't it?'

" 'Not everything,' replied the judge. 'Here is an absolute contract of sale, entered into by Mr. Armstrong during his lifetime with his two brothers. The three of them were in good health at the time. They all passed excellent examinations and were insured for $40,000 each. No one knew who was going to die first. They agreed on a price they thought was fair. Here it is, $80,000, set right in the agreement. Here are their signatures. This is an absolute contract of sale to take effect upon death. Let me give you an illustration: I have here a thermos jug (holding up the thermos jug) which my wife gave to me last Christmas. She paid $100 for it. I wouldn't pay any such price for a thermos jug, but that's what she paid for it. Suppose I entered into an agreement this minute with you . . . put it into writing . . . that in the event of my death, I hereby sell this jug to you for $10. Now I die . . . you go to my widow and offer to pay her $10, but she refuses to accept it. That would be foolish, because I actually sold the jug to you under a binding contract of sale to take effect immediately and automatically upon my death. My widow has nothing to do with the sale. The sale has already been completed, and there's nothing for her to do but receive the money.'

"The lawyer said: 'Your Honor, this man drew $18,000 a year salary plus profits out of the business. Now they are offering his widow the equivalent of only *four years' salary!* Is that fair?'

"Judge Patterson answered: 'His *salary* had nothing to do with the value of the business. That was money earned for *services* rendered, just the same as any other employee. The salary of any employee terminates at death, unless some written agreement provides otherwise.'

"The case was thrown out of court. Judge Patterson closed by saying: 'The Orphans' Court is two years behind with just such cases, and it is a waste of time and a waste of your client's money to go on with endless arguments when there can be only *one* result. This court, or any court, has no power to add or subtract words that will change the meaning of a man's will, or a contract he made during his lifetime. We can add words in order to clarify the obvious meaning—but never to change the meaning or intent of the document. . . .'

"The next day, I went to see Judge Patterson. I told him I was on the Speaker's Committee of the Life Underwriters' Association, that most of the speakers we had were either life insurance salesmen or executives. 'You could do a lot of good, Judge Patterson, helping to prevent needless law suits you see going through your court every day,' I suggested. 'Won't you come talk to us? Tell us about some of these cases . . . and how we can help prevent them?'

"The Judge said, 'I shall be very glad to.'

"He was the speaker at our next meeting. His talk was superb! It did so much good for us, because he gave exciting action pictures of cases going through the courts. We saw what should have been done; the mistakes and oversights of partners and corporations; their failure to have *any* agreement; or where they had the 'old-time' agreement, giving surviving partners the 'option' or the 'right,' in the event of death, to buy the deceased's interest at book value.

"Judge Patterson showed how *meaningless* such agreements are, and why they so frequently result in bitter fights. ' "Option," or "right," means just what it says,' the Judge told us. 'If the surviving partners decide not to exercise the option, nobody can force them to do it. If the widow or heirs of the deceased do not want to accept the offer, it is likewise optional with them.'

"Judge Patterson recommended that all partners, and owners of close corporations should have an agreement binding to *all* parties, and that the sale price should be stated right in the body of the agreement or a schedule attached thereto and made part of the agreement. The price should be reviewed at least once every year and changed accordingly. 'In some businesses where the price may be fluctuating constantly, due to inventory, etc.,' the Judge said, 'there should be a formula stated in the agreement prescribing how a fair price can be set in the event of a death.'

"That night Judge Patterson made us all realize, as we never had before, how important a part life insurance played. In most cases, *indispensable*. 'Many of the fights in court would never have occurred,' the Judge emphasized, 'if life insurance had been carried, making it possible for the survivors to carry out the terms of the agreement.' "

The entire time I was telling these four officers of that company this story, they never once interrupted me. I never had a more interested and attentive audience.

I was with them altogether *four hours!* The interview started shortly after eleven o'clock. At one o'clock the president said, "Let's go get some lunch and come back afterward and resume this conference."

During lunch, I said nothing about insurance. Neither did they. We returned to the office, and about three o'clock I thought all but one seemed ready for the close so I said: "Gentlemen, there are four steps in working out a plan of this kind." (I always count the four steps with my fingers.)

"The *first* step is the examination to find out if you are all insurable. If any of you are uninsurable, we may have to do this a different way. So the examination is the first step.

"The *second* step is for you to set the purchase price: how much you would consider a fair value of this business, the value you would be willing to sell for in the event of your death. You will be thinking this over, while the insurance company is thinking *you* over.

"The *third* step is for you to decide on how much of this valuation you will insure. That will depend largely, I suppose, on how much the insurance costs. I will be prepared to give you these figures a few days after your examinations are completed.

"The *fourth* step is the agreement. (I always put great emphasis on this, because the prospects will try to make this the first step if you don't cover it thoroughly.) The fourth step is the agreement, and that usually takes a lot of time. Attorneys work slowly, as you probably know (with a smile)."

That afternoon, they agreed to be examined. I succeeded in selling them what turned out to be the largest sale I had ever made up to that time. Their 10/15th stock and the life insurance were placed in escrow with a trust company, under an agreement.

Now, how did I have the courage to go up there that morning without Mr. Hunsicker and sell those four men, nearly twice my age? *Stories!* It was the stories that gave me courage and confidence. Without them I wouldn't even have *considered* attempting to sell them alone. But I *knew* I could tell them the stories; and I *knew* those stories fitted their situation. And it was the *stories* that sold those men more than a half million dollars of life insurance!

By the time I came down to the close, the "four steps," three of the four men were ready and *wanted* to go ahead.

When only one of them started to put up resistance at this point, I just kept quiet and let the other three sell him.

SUMMED UP

Rule Number One to Conquer Fear

1. The most important rule I ever found to conquer fear and develop courage and self-confidence is to: *"Do the thing you fear to do; and keep on doing it until you get a record of successful experiences behind you."*
If I hadn't remembered that rule, I never would have gone up there alone that morning and attempted to interview those four big men.

2. As all four of these successful men nearly twice my age came in that room and sat down, I was terribly nervous. But I had made up my mind to make this *the most enthusiastic interview I ever had!* Did it work? It worked like magic. Two things happened:
   (a) My enthusiasm almost entirely overcame my fear. In fact, my nervousness worked *for* me, and it was by far the best interview I had ever had.
   (b) My enthusiasm and excitement affected these stable, older men, and they too became excited.

3. How do you learn to tell stories well? By telling stories. After you have told a story a few times, you'll find yourself improving with each telling. You'll eliminate all needless words and details. You will make it march! You'll get excited. If your story

gives your listener an idea that will help him make money, or solve some problem of his, *he* will get excited, and *you* will do business!

4. *The Four Steps:* I find that men love those four steps. It makes it simple and easy for them to understand, and easy to do.
They only have to take *one* step at a time.
And they remember it that way.

30.

*An Amazing Story
That Has Helped Me
Close Many Big Sales*

THE OTHER DAY a good friend of mine, vice-president of a manufacturing concern, called me on the phone and said: "Frank, we have been talking about increasing our life insurance under our business insurance agreement. When can you come down and talk with us about it?"

A phone call like that at one time might have brought on a heart attack, but now? ... Well, I made it down there in fifteen minutes!

I didn't make a *sale*. I just listened and took the *order!*

Now why have I mentioned this? Because the situation which brought about that easy sale never would have happened if I hadn't told the following story to the founders of that company many years before. Here is the story:

"One time I was talking with Robert M. Green, president of Robert M. Green and Sons, Inc., America's oldest soda fountain manufacturers, about a plan for the protection and perpetuation of his company. He listened for awhile with real interest, then interrupted me and said: 'Do you want to hear a story that will be a big help to you in selling your idea to businessmen?' I said, 'You've got me all excited before you start. What is the story?'

" 'Many years ago, I was living in a small two-story row house

up a side street not far from the Baldwin Locomotive plant,'
said Mr. Green. 'Next door to us lived a young couple with two
small children. Every evening, the husband came home from
the locomotive works, dressed in dirty, greasy overalls; face
black with coal dirt, carrying a tin dinner pail.

" 'A few years before this, it seems that the seven partners of
the Baldwin Locomotive Works held a special meeting. Mr.
Baldwin said: "Gentlemen, we believe our business has un-
bounded possibilities. If it is going to grow and make the prog-
ress we visualize, we must keep the ownership in the hands of
those actively running the business."

" 'As the result of that meeting, an agreement was drawn, a
simple little agreement in which there was a contract of sale,
binding the seven partners, in the event of the death of any one,
to buy the deceased member's interest. They placed a valuation
on the business—that value to be revised upon the closing of
the books at the end of each fiscal year. Heirs of the deceased
could not contest the sale, because the agreement provided that
the sale was to take place automatically upon the death of any
partner.

" 'A few years after that agreement was entered into, a partner named Tomlinson died. His share of the partnership shown
on the last closing of the books had increased to $250,000. The
surviving partners paid his estate off, then looked around their
organization for a younger man to take Tomlinson's place. But
they couldn't find the right man.

" 'However, there was a young man they'd had their eyes on
for some time. He worked around Baldwin's plant a great deal
for the Pennsylvania Railroad. His job was to inspect and
approve every engine before delivery to the railroad.

" 'They offered Tomlinson's interest to him for $250,000. *He
almost dropped dead!* "I have no money," he said. "I'm only
making $150 a month!"

" 'They said, "We don't want your money. *We want you!*"
They took his note for $250,000, and in a remarkably few years
he paid off those notes out of his share of the profits.

" 'That man finally became president of the Baldwin Locomotive Works. His name? *Samuel Vauclain*. He was the same young man who lived next door to us whom we used to see coming home every night looking like a coal miner!

"This was such a terrific story, I wanted to be sure I had it right, so a few days after Mr. Green told me the story, I was able to get an interview with Samuel Vauclain in his office at the Baldwin Locomotive Works. I asked him if that story was true. He said, 'Absolutely!' He even repeated in greater detail the story Mr. Green had told me. I asked him some questions and here are his answers, which he seemed perfectly willing to give to me."

ME. Mr. Vauclain, would you mind telling me whether these partners ever carried partnership insurance?

VAUCLAIN. Oh my, yes. As our business grew, we kept buying more and more life insurance, until we were said to be one of the most heavily insured partnerships in the world. But our insurance never cost anything.

ME. Why? (*I asked it in surprise.*)

VAUCLAIN. In 1907, there was a money panic. All the banks closed, and you couldn't get any money. *Cash* was selling at a big premium. Baldwin's had contracts with nations all over the world. Our contracts called for delivery of locomotives within a stipulated number of days. Upon failure to make delivery, there was a heavy penalty for every day we went beyond the date of the contract. We would have lost more money that year than *all* the money we ever paid out over the years for insurance premiums. But we were able to keep our entire plant going, paying our employees in cash every Saturday night, because the life insurance companies were in a position to advance us our entire payroll! By keeping our employees happy and paying them off every Saturday night, Baldwin's was able to meet the *deadline* on all those contracts!

ME. That's a wonderful story, Mr. Vauclain, I wish every employer in America could hear it. . . . Mr. Vauclain, how long did Baldwin's operate as a partnership?

VAUCLAIN. Until 1910.

ME. Is that so? Why did you incorporate?

VAUCLAIN. By 1910, we had grown to such proportions, we had to borrow great sums of money. We found it necessary to float bond issues, preferred and common stock, through bankers in New York. To make this possible, we simply had to incorporate.

ME. After you incorporated, were your officers able to maintain controlling majority of the stock?

VAUCLAIN. No, indeed. That was impossible after the common stock got out on the open market.

ME. What about these young men you brought into the business—as you were taken in yourself years ago. Are you still able to follow that policy?

VAUCLAIN. We still follow that principle exactly as Mr. Baldwin started it. We keep our eyes open for promising young material in our organization all the time. *They're the life blood of any business!*

"I asked Mr. Vauclain if he would be willing to speak some night at our Underwriters' Dinner. He said he would be glad to.

"He proved to be a wonderful speaker! He held us spellbound for two hours that night. I am sure his talk did more to inspire us to go out and render greater service to businessmen than any talk we heard that year by any life insurance salesmen."

This Samuel Vauclain story has helped me sell millions of dollars of business insurance!
After all these years, I get just as much thrill out of telling the story as I did the first time I heard Mr. Vauclain tell it himself. Even today, I get so excited when I tell it, I often get emotional and can hardly go on with the story.

I wish every salesman in the life insurance business would help to tell this story to the world! After you tell it a few times, you will get just as excited over it as I have.

I've found it a hundred times more effective in selling business insurance than any complicated legal rulings I might quote, or any preaching I could do!

I remember reading one time how Thomas Edison, in 1879, turned a glowing loop of carbonized thread from his wife's sewing basket into a miracle of light. As this first electric "lamp" burned briefly on his laboratory table, Edison envisioned "great cities lighted from central stations; a vast system of machines and wires which would bring light to city streets, stores, office buildings and homes."

Most people thought this was just a wild dream, but Thomas Edison lived to see his dream come true.

Only a few days after I read this story, right while I was working on this chapter, I walked by City Hall in Philadelphia on the way over to the station to catch a train for home. On the north plaza, facing Broad Street, I noticed a large bronze statue. I had passed that statue hundreds of times before but never really *looked* at it. This time, as I looked up, I saw the name:

BALDWIN

I stopped short and stood there several moments. Then I walked around back of it to see if there was any inscription. Inscribed on the back of the figure were these words:

MATTHIAS WILLIAM BALDWIN

Founder of the Baldwin Locomotive Works
 His Skill in the Mechanic Arts
His Faithful Discharge of the Duties of
 Citizenship His Broad Philanthrophy
And Unfailing Benevolence And
 His Devotion to All Christian Work
Placed Him Foremost Among the Makers
 of Philadelphia

As I reread this profound tribute, I realized that few private citizens ever have been honored by a big city with such a permanent and perpetual memorial.

Then I thought of the Samuel Vauclain story I was writing about. I thought: "It *would* take a man with Baldwin's vision to give birth to such a Great American Ideal—for the Baldwin Locomotive Works was probably the world's first business establishment to create an ownership management plan funded by life insurance, to guarantee the perpetuation and the protection of its business!"

While this was a different kind of vision from the one Edison had about that time, yet it had to be a man with the same kind of foresight and vision.

As I stood there, I meditated on the important role Clayt Hunsicker had played as a life insurance salesman in pioneering this idea and on the rapidly increasing contribution it is making to the American way of life.

My thoughts went back to the time when I, a raw beginner, who never finished grade school, became associated with a man like Hunsicker. If I had known then the important role this idea would play in American business, I never would have had the nerve to go up and speak to Clayt that day when he agreed to let me act as his "bird dog."

I got all choked up with emotion, thinking that a little guy like me could have played even a small part in such a great work. Tears dropped off my cheeks as I turned away and walked toward Suburban Station.

31.

He Wanted to Drop $25,000, But This Idea Sold Him $150,000 More

A CLIENT OF MINE, sixty-four years of age, called me on the phone one day and asked: "How long are you going to be there?"

I said: "Do you want to tell me what you have in mind? I might be able to save you some time."

"I want to *see* you," said he. "I have to drop some of my insurance. I am now drawing only half pay after taxes, and paying $4,100 for my insurance. When I was getting full pay that was all right . . . but not now!"

When he arrived in my office I said, "Mr. Stortz, when you bought this insurance, you had a definite need for it, didn't you?"

"Yes, I did," he answered.

"That need still exists, doesn't it?"

"Yes, but I haven't the income to carry it now," he said firmly.

"Must you get the cash out of these policies, or is it just the cost of carrying them that worries you?"

"No, I don't need cash, but I must cut my expenses down so that I can live within my income," he declared.

"You mean your *present* income?"

"Yes, we aren't making money in our business now, and with taxes the way they are, I don't see the prospects of making any money in the near future," Mr. Stortz explained.

"But a year from now, Mr. Stortz, if your business justifies it, you might be able to carry this insurance—isn't that a possibility?"

"Oh, it's a possibility," he agreed.

"*Good!* Then, let me make this suggestion: why don't you borrow enough on the insurance to pay for it another year? A year from now, if you find you must drop it, you can still get back almost as much money as you can get today. In the meantime, you'll have this protection which you need worse *today* than when you first took it, isn't that right?"

"And I don't have to pay anything now?" he asked, surprised.

"Not a dollar," I assured him.

He agreed and seemed very happy with the idea. After we got that out of the way, I said, "Mr. Stortz, who is going to run that business down there if anything happens to you?"

STORTZ. Why, the president, Harry Schmidt.

ME. Suppose Harry should die first; who is going to run the business?

STORTZ. I suppose I will.

ME. What? With two hundred shares of stock out of 2800 you are going to run that business? Women and children will own 2600 shares of that stock, represented by lawyers; *minor* children must be represented by a separate set of lawyers. . . . How important is Harry Schmidt in that business?

STORTZ. He is recognized as one of the top men in the paper box industry.

ME. Then, if anything happens to him, all his responsibilities fall on your shoulders on top of what you already have, is that right?

STORTZ. Yes, that's right.

ME. Do you think you could handle a situation like that with only 200 shares of stock? Harry's salary would stop at his death. With him gone, the business would probably lose money and his family would get no return from their investment. What's going to happen? The whole thing will be blamed on you! They'll probably declare you are too old to run the business.

With their large majority, they can vote you out of your job. Isn't that right, Mr. Stortz?

STORTZ. I have often thought of that. But what can we do about it?

ME. The corporation should insure Harry Schmidt's life for the full amount of his interest in the business so that, in the event of his death, you survivors would have complete control and his heirs would be paid off in cash.

STORTZ. That's a wonderful idea, but we can't afford to pay the premiums on a large amount of insurance like that.

ME. Mr. Stortz, that's just the reason I am talking to you about this. In fact, that is the *only* reason I am talking to you about it. If this business were making a lot of money, Harry Schmidt might not want to give up this investment for his estate.

STORTZ. Well, it is a splendid idea and I'll talk to him about it.

ME. No, don't do that, that's *my* job. Let *me* do that.

STORTZ. All right, I wish you would.

ME. Look, Mr. Stortz (*as I walked out to the elevator with him*), if you don't mind, I would rather you didn't say anything to Harry about my having talked with you about this . . . you can understand why it would be better. He may get the impression that you are talking for your own selfish benefit. With his owning 80 per cent of the stock, don't you think it would be better for him to feel that I am talking to him first?

STORTZ. Yes, you are right. I won't say a word.

I immediately got in touch with the president and made an appointment to see him the next day about a matter which I told him was very important. In our interview, I said, "Harry, if anything should happen . . ." and I reversed the whole story from *his* standpoint: "Do you think it is fair? You have been plowing money all your life back into this business; almost your entire estate is in this business. You are worth much more around here than you give yourself credit for. I know. I have talked to some of your employees, I have talked with some of your competitors. They tell me you are one of the leading men in the paper box industry. If anything happens to you, how in the world is Mr. Stortz, a man sixty-four years old, going to take over all your responsibility? The chances are, this business wouldn't survive five years after your death. Your investment would be *wiped out!* All this money you have put back into your business, and the sacrifices you are making now, would be *lost!* Is it fair for you to let your estate be tied up in such an uncertain investment? It is all right while you are alive, but in case of your death, for your family . . . what then?"

SCHMIDT. I have thought of it many times but I don't know what to do about it.

ME. That's why I am here—in fact, that is the *only* reason I am here to talk to you. There is only *one* solution: the corporation must insure your life for the full amount of your interest, or as much of it as possible, so that if anything happens to you, your family will not suffer. They will be guaranteed a safe, steady income directly through life insurance.

SCHMIDT. I believe you're right. I'll take it up with Mr. Stortz and the others right away.

ME. *No.* Don't do that. That's my business. Let *me* do that. Don't you see, Harry, they might get the wrong impression, think it is very selfish of you to want the company to put out as much money as it would require to pay off your entire interest in this business. First, let me have you examined to find out whether you would be able to get this much insurance. If you are uninsurable right now, or, if we can't get sufficient insurance to cover your interest, we may have to work it out in a different way. So let's have the examination made first. Then let *me* talk to your associates. That's my job. *Right?*

SCHMIDT. Well, all right.

ME. Harry, if you don't mind, I would rather you'd not mention to Mr. Stortz that I have spoken to you about this. . . . Is that all right?

SCHMIDT. I see what you mean.

Well, now, if you think that sounds tricky, would you be interested to know where I got that approach? I got it from one of the world's greatest salesmen, *Benjamin Franklin!* The University of Pennsylvania, the Pennsylvania Hospital, the Public Library of Philadelphia, and many other wonderful projects in Philadelphia and all over the world are still going strong today, over a century and a half after his death, because Franklin used that kind of diplomacy *to do good!* And he wrote about it in his *Autobiography,* he felt it was so important.

Explaining this psychology, Franklin wrote: ". . . thus it worked both ways" . . . "After thinking of it, I more easily excused myself for having made some use of cunning."

As I was leaving this paper box manufacturer, I said: "Harry, before I talk with Mr. Stortz, this is one of four steps in the plan.

"First, the examination. It would embarrass you if I spoke to Mr. Stortz first, then found you were not able to pass the physical."

The examinations were made, Mr. Schmidt was approved, but I was able to get only $150,000 issued.

An appointment was made. As we sat down in the president's office, I handed Mr. Schmidt and Mr. Stortz each an original copy of my letter outlining the plan. I held the yellow carbon copy, then said:

"Now if you don't mind, I am just going to sit here quietly while you read this."

Here is an exact copy of the letter:

HENRY SCHMIDT & BRO. INC.
328 Vine Street
PHILADELPHIA, PENNSYLVANIA

Gentlemen:

After giving considerable thought concerning the protection and perpetuation of the business of Henry Schmidt & Bro., Inc., we beg to submit the following plan for your earnest consideration.

Established in 1887, your business has always been owner-managed. The original founders of the business have passed on, and now 2400 out of 3000 shares of stock are held by Mr. Harry H. Schmidt. His death would mean a loss to your business and to his dependents. To his dependents it is a very serious loss, because his salary stops immediately; they could not sell or borrow on the stock; and the chances of dividends being paid in the future are quite uncertain.

This always brings distress to the heirs of the deceased and in turn frequently causes great pressure, legal and otherwise, upon those who are left to run the business. Both sides at interest need and deserve every possible protection.

The only safe way to accomplish this is through business life insurance and a properly drawn stock purchase agreement. Let us assume, for example, the present value is $90.00 per share. Mr. Schmidt's 2400 shares would be worth $216,000.00. To insure Mr. Schmidt's life for that sum, at the present time, would probably require too great an outlay. Therefore, we have issued $150,000.00 of insurance on his life. The cost of this would be taken care of by the corporation just the same as the fire insurance and other overhead expenses.

Now, in the event of Mr. Schmidt's death, the insurance company will immediately pay $150,000.00. This would leave a balance of $66,000.00 for the corporation to pay to Mr. Schmidt's estate, which could be covered by interest bearing notes to be amortized monthly over a period of years.

Part of the service we render is to co-operate with your attorney for the proper drawing of the agreement and arranging for any changes that may be necessary from year to year such as selling price, etc.

There are four steps to take in arranging this plan:

1. The insurance examination.
2. Present valuation of your stock.
3. The amount of insurance the corporation will take to cover Mr. Schmidt's interest.
4. The business insurance stock purchase agreement.

You have taken the first step. We would urge that you immediately put into force as much insurance as you feel the corporation can afford; and the next two steps are a matter of detail which we will then be able to work out promptly.

The foregoing plan is now recognized as the best method to protect and perpetuate a business, and is rapidly being adopted by leading close corporations and partnerships throughout the country. Through this plan of ownership management, there is no reason why this old, established business of Henry Schmidt & Bro., Inc., cannot be perpetuated for many generations to come.

Very respectfully yours,

Frank Bettger

Finally, the president spoke up: "I think this is something the company ought to do. If anything happens to me, I would want you men to have control of the business without any interference."

Mr. Stortz asked: "Where are we going to get the money to pay for all this insurance?"

Then they looked at me.

I said: "Where do you get the money to meet your payroll each week? . . . How much is your payroll running?"

Mr. Stortz answered, "About $1,800 a week."

I said, "In other words, about $90,000 a year, is that right?"

"Yes, that's about right."

"If you sent for your bookkeeper right now, and he told you the payroll was running $96,000 a year, would you be alarmed?"

"No," answered Mr. Stortz.

"If he told you it was only running $84,000 a year, would you be highly elated?"

"No," nodded Stortz.

"Then, why not look at this insurance the same as your payroll? Why not think of it as another employee you are putting on, the most valuable employee you ever hired? He is going to give you this protection you need so badly. At the end of say ten years, if you do not have the same need for it, this employee is going to return to you approximately two-thirds of the money you paid him. In other words, this is not a *cost*, it's an *investment!*"

Mr. Schmidt asked, "Suppose the time should come that we *couldn't* pay these premiums?"

"Harry," I assured him, "it would pay to do this, even if you had to sell some assets, some of the company's securities. That would merely be a transfer of assets!"

I received a substantial check in part payment of the annual premium, and they paid the balance within sixty days.

MAGIC PHRASES

"Mr. Stortz, who is going to run this business if anything happens to you?"

"Mr. Stortz, that's just the reason I am talking to you about this. In fact, that is the ONLY *reason I am talking to you about it.*

(I find this a powerful way to meet the chief objection.)

When they say: "It's a good idea. I'll talk to my partner about it":
"No, don't do that—that's MY *job. Let* ME *do that."*

When they say: "Where do we get the money to pay for this?":
"Where do you get the money to meet your payroll each week? . . . How much is your payroll running?"
When they state the amount of payroll, I simply add my item to it and show how insignificant it would be. Note that I always do this with questions, never positive statements. Then I say:
"Why not look at this the same as your payroll? Why not think of it as another employee you are putting on, the most valuable employee you ever hired?"

Why wouldn't it pay you to do this, even if you had to sell some assets—some of the company's securities? That would merely be a transfer of assets!

32.

They Weren't Interested,
Until These Ideas
Made Them Want to Buy

ONE DAY I CALLED on two friends of mine, owners of a medium sized knit goods manufacturing business. I was surprised to see several improvements they had made in their plant since I had been there only a few months previously.

I didn't sell them additional insurance that day, but when I left there I had cards of introduction to all three contractors who did the alteration jobs.

The following week I dropped in, without an appointment, on the plumbing and heating contractors. We'll call them Connor & Taylor. Mr. Connor was in his office, and the girl said I could go right in. Here is the interview that took place:

SCENE 1

ME. Mr. Connor?

CONNOR. Yes.

ME. My name is Bettger, Frank Bettger, of the Fidelity Mutual Life Insurance Company. Your friend, Bill Stafford, asked me to stop in and see you the next time I was in your neighborhood. Can you talk for a few minutes now, or would you rather I call later? (*As I said this, I handed him the card of introduction.*)

CONNOR. Good heavens, man. You're wasting your time! I'm no insurance prospect. I'm too old to be thinking of anything like that again. I'm lucky if I can keep what insurance I've got.

183

ME. Mr. Connor, would you say that Mr. Stafford is a man of good business judgment?

CONNOR. Certainly.

ME. Would you say he is the kind of man who would intentionally give you a bad steer?

CONNOR. No, I don't believe he would.

ME. *Good.* Mr. Stafford wants me to tell you about the situation he and his partner were confronted with. He thinks there is a possibility that you and your partner may have a similar situation. Do you have enough confidence in Mr. Stafford's judgment to take ten minutes to find out about this?

CONNOR. Yes, of course. Go ahead.

ME. First, Mr. Connor, I am going to ask you some very private questions, but understand, if anybody ever knows anything about what you tell me it will be because *you* tell them—not because *I* do. It is in strict confidence. Right?

CONNOR. *Right!*

(Let me repeat: I never remove the questionnaire from my pocket until the prospect begins answering my questions. And I put the paper back in my pocket in the same manner—while he is answering my last question. I never show it to him in the first interview. As soon as the agreed-upon time is up, I usually rise and say: "Well, my ten minutes are up. Is there anything else you would like to tell me, Mr. Connor?" . . . Then I get out as soon as I can.)

ME. Thank you for your confidence, Mr. Connor. (*I shook hands with him for the first time.*) Remember, if anybody ever knows anything about what you've told me, it will be because *you* tell them, not because *I* do. It's in strict confidence. *Right?*

CONNOR. Right!

ME. When I come back, Mr. Connor, I would like you to have your partner, Mr. Taylor, sit in with us. Can you give me some idea when you will both be here together?

CONNOR. Well, Mr. Taylor is our outside man and it's hard to catch him here in the office, except Friday afternoons . . . that's pay day.

ME. Could we set next Friday afternoon, say about 3:30?

CONNOR. Better make it 4:00. And you'd better phone me Friday morning to make sure.

ME. *Fine*. Thank you very much!

SCENE 2

Telephone Conversation
Friday Morning

ME. Mr. Connor?

CONNOR. Yes.

ME. This is Frank Bettger, friend of Bill Stafford. Is that appointment all right for you and Mr. Taylor this afternoon?

CONNOR. Oh, Mr. Bettger. Why ... uh ... I mentioned that to Mr. Taylor and he doesn't see any sense in taking a lot of time talking about insurance. We are busy, and what's the use of talking about something we are not the slightest bit interested in?

ME. Mr. Connor, you *are* interested in your *business*, aren't you?

CONNOR. Sure.

ME. Well, that is exactly what I am going to talk to you about —your business. You gave me some information the other day that revealed a situation you and Mr. Taylor face, and you should do something about it.

CONNOR. But boiled down, you are going to try to sell us some insurance, isn't that right?

ME. Mr. Connor, I want you to distinctly understand that, as the result of our interview this afternoon, you are not going to be asked to buy life insurance. You and your partner face a problem and I am going to show you two methods of meeting that problem.

CONNOR. How much time will it take?

ME. That depends on how much you and Mr. Taylor talk. It won't take me fifteen minutes to give you the information.

CONNOR. Well, suppose you get here about 4:40.

ME. Good. I'll be there.

SCENE 3

Final Interview
Friday Afternoon

Mr. Connor introduced me to his partner, Mr. Taylor, then we all sat down. Without any preliminary remarks, I handed each of them a bound copy of the plan I had drawn up for them. I kept the unbound carbon copy for myself. There was total silence as the three of us read our copies through. Here is an exact copy of the plan:

CONNOR & TAYLOR

BUSINESS PERPETUATION PLAN

The following thoughts suggest what we would consider to be the best method for you to adopt for the protection and perpetuation of your business.

You, Mr. Connor and Mr. Taylor, can, of course, make much more satisfactory arrangements between yourselves now while you are both living and in good health than can your widows or your executors.

The law of the Commonwealth of Pennsylvania governing business partnerships states clearly that the death of a partner terminates the partnership. In the absence of an express agreement to the contrary, every partnership is dissolved by the death of a partner.

Established in 1927, your business has grown and prospered. You are operating as a partnership, but your agreement makes no provision to protect each other in the event one of you should die. This is not an unusual oversight where two or more men have confidence in each other as you have. But this is a dangerous situation.

Therefore, we would suggest that you immediately include in your agreement a contract of sale binding the survivor to buy, and the estate to sell, automatically in the event one of you should die. The sale price should be named in the agreement. This price should be reviewed from time to time, not less than once a year, increased or decreased as your business justifies it. Life insurance should be carried on each of you covering the entire value of each partner's interest or as much of it as is practical.

If the life insurance is not sufficient to provide the full amount, then the agreement should give the survivor the privilege of amortizing the balance with interest bearing notes, payable monthly over a period of two or three years.

Disposing of your interest in the business cannot be *properly* covered in your Will.

By this agreement, control of the business remains exactly where it should. The surviving partner can proceed easily, without stress or worry, under the terms of the agreement which he made with his deceased partner during his lifetime. No negotiations are necessary.

No outsiders can interfere. The sale price and all other terms of transfer are fixed in the agreement. All has been attended to and the business can go on uninterrupted. The surviving partner thus is in a position to take in one or two junior partners if necessary or advisable for the protection and continuity of the business.

The widow and children of the deceased partner are assured a fair and prompt settlement for their share of interest in the business. They are not faced with danger of loss or shrinkage. They will have an immediate and uninterrupted income. Your widow is not burdened by any business responsibility whatsoever.

The estate of the deceased is free from any possible liability.

The chance of friction between the family of the deceased and the surviving partner is entirely eliminated.

The foregoing plan is now generally recognized as the best method to protect and perpetuate a business enterprise and is rapidly being adopted by partnerships and close corporations throughout the country.

Through this plan of maintaining ownership in the hands of active partners, there is no reason why the business of Connor & Taylor cannot be perpetuated for many generations to come.

. . . After they finished reading, they looked up and waited for me to talk. But I waited for them:

TAYLOR. How do you mean, Mr. Bettger, that the death of one of us would dissolve our partnership? If one of us should die, couldn't the other one go on and run the business?

ME. Not unless you have a written agreement to take care of the problems created by the death.

TAYLOR. What do you mean, problems?

ME. *Dead* men can't be partners. If you have no buy and sell agreement, the surviving partner finds himself involved, *the next day*, winding up the affairs of the partnership. One of his first duties is the collection of monies owed the firm. A valuation must be placed on all equipment such as tools, machinery, material, trucks, real estate, office equipment, etc. Up to the day of his death, the deceased partner drew an income out of the business. His family will no longer be able to draw *any* income. The surviving partner has no authority to make any payments to them until he has closed out the business. This always creates dissatisfaction and suspicion.

CONNOR. Did Stafford Bros. have an agreement drawn up?

ME. Yes. That's why they sent me here to see you and Mr. Taylor.

TAYLOR. I could raise the money at the bank and buy Mr. Connor's interest if anything should happen to him.

ME. Maybe you could, Mr. Taylor, but if you did, you would have to pay the bank back both *principal* and *interest*. Isn't that right?

TAYLOR. Certainly.

ME. All right. Let's examine that plan for a minute: Mr. Connor told me he values his interest at $60,000. In the event of his death, you will borrow $60,000 from the bank. Let's assume the bank agrees to let you pay off your loan over a period of six years at the rate of $10,000 a year, plus interest. First, you may find that you can't draw $10,000 additional if Mr. Connor dies, because you must employ an assistant at say $6,000 a year. Then, with your increased income of about $20,000 you find your taxes greatly increased. If you pay $10,000 to the bank and pay your taxes, you will have *almost nothing left to live on!*

TAYLOR. What else can we do?

ME. If you knew of a plan where you pay only interest, and never have to pay back any principal, would that be good business?

TAYLOR (*looking very skeptical*). What do you mean by that?

ME. Look. Here's all you do. You two men will have a Buy-and-Sell Agreement funded with life insurance. Now, upon the death of either partner, your insurance automatically provides the money to make your agreement absolutely effective, without your ever paying any principal. *You never pay anything but interest!*

CONNOR. How much would that interest amount to?

ME. Only 3½ per cent.

CONNOR. Three and a half per cent of what?

ME. You value your interest in this business at $60,000. If you insure the full value of both your and Mr. Taylor's interest, that would be 3½ per cent of $120,000—or $4,200.

CONNOR. We can't afford it.

ME. Why not?

CONNOR. We don't have the money to carry any such amount of insurance.

ME. (*Pause*) In addition to that, Mr. Connor, isn't there some other reason in the back of your mind?

CONNOR. No. That's all. We can't afford it.

ME. I'm glad you brought that up at this time. You are going to be surprised how *little* it will actually cost you. You will pay *nothing* out of your pocket. It is merely a bookkeeping item. Your partnership carries a very substantial average bank balance. All you do is transfer a portion of your bank account to your insurance account. This benefits you immediately. It builds up the firm's credit, because banks, bonding companies and other creditors will know that the firm of Connor & Taylor will not be interrupted by death. Each year, as you build up your insurance account, it gives both of you a safe and convenient savings, guaranteed whether you live or die.

CONNOR. All right, Mr. Bettger, Mr. Taylor and I will think it over and if we decide to do anything about it, we'll get in touch with you.

ME. Mr. Connor, you remember I told you, as the result of this talk, I would not ask you and Mr. Taylor to buy any life insurance. My job is to help you find the best way to solve your problem. There is no doubt in your mind that you want Mr. Taylor to have full control of the business without interference from outsiders, if anything happens to you, is there?

CONNOR. No, that's the way I would want it.

ME. Mr. Taylor, is there any doubt in your mind that you want Mr. Connor to take over the business if you should go first?

TAYLOR. No, my wife doesn't know anything about this business.

ME. Then you and Mr. Connor don't have to think that over, do you?

TAYLOR. No, I guess we don't have to think that over.

ME. Mr. Connor, is it all right to talk plain in front of Mr. Taylor about some of these figures you gave me last week?

CONNOR. Yes, go right ahead. There is nothing about my affairs he doesn't already know.

ME. You frankly confessed to me as we went through these questions that it would be necessary for your wife to have $300 monthly in the event of your death. Does that figure still hold?

CONNOR. Yes, that's right.

ME. You don't have to think that over, do you?

CONNOR. No, that's right.

ME. You frankly told me you would want your wife to have your home clear of any mortgage, is that correct?

CONNOR. Yes, I told you that.

ME. You told me you couldn't retire at sixty-five on less than $700 monthly, is that right?

CONNOR. I don't know how I could retire on that today.

ME. *Right!* Now, by the simple process of transferring only a part of the firm's bank account to the insurance account, you and Mr. Taylor immediately transfer all this risk to the *insurance* company! Merely by a bookkeeping process you accomplish your objectives—immediately! Isn't that wonderful? . . . There's only one thing wrong with it.

CONNOR. What's that?

ME. I don't know whether you can get it. Is there any question in your minds as to whether you will be able to pass the physical examination for life insurance?

CONNOR. Well, I haven't taken insurance for several years, but I think I could pass. I've never been sick.

ME. *Good.* How about you, Mr. Taylor?

TAYLOR. Oh, I think I can pass all right.

ME. *Fine.* Now, there are four steps for you to take: *First,* the physical examination. If you should not be insurable you may have to work this out through your bank; the *second* step is for you to set a price on the present value of your business. The *third* step is for you to decide how much of this valuation you will insure. The *fourth* step is the agreement. The agreement usually takes a lot of time, because, as you probably know, lawyers work slowly. Let's take the first step and see whether you men are as good on the inside as you look on the *outside*. How about tomorrow? If I have Dr. Van Dervoort here tomorrow morning about 10:15, will that be all right?

TAYLOR. Well, I think Mr. Connor and I should think this over before we decide to go ahead with the insurance.

ME. That's right. And the *first* step in thinking it over is to get examined and find out whether you can pass. Isn't that right?

CONNOR. Let's see. Tomorrow is Saturday. I'll be here in the morning. Were you coming in tomorrow, Howard?

TAYLOR. Yes. I've got to finish figuring the bid on that Blankin job.

I had them approved for $60,000 apiece. The contracts were issued and they bought the entire amount with annual premiums totalling $4,190. A few days before, $120,000 seemed like a fabulous amount of life insurance for them to buy.

I never close a difficult sale that I don't think of the time I went down to Atlantic City years ago to find out how that master "closer" Billy Walker did it. Again I see old Billy's wonderful smile, and I hear him say:

"When a man offers objections, he doesn't mean he won't buy. What he really means is that you haven't convinced him yet. You haven't produced enough evidence to make him want to buy!"

ANALYSIS OF THE CONNOR-TAYLOR SALE

The "bull's-eye": Note there are thirty-seven questions I asked in that sale. Every question kept shooting straight for the *target.* And the bull's-eye was *not* insurance. It *never* is. That goes for *anything* you want to sell. If you discuss some vital problem with a person, he is anxious to talk with an open mind about any idea that may help him solve that problem.

Connor and Taylor were definitely not interested in wasting time listening to a salesman try to sell them insurance. But they were *vitally* interested when I pointed out a problem; and they listened with great interest when I showed them the two methods they could use to solve that problem. I discussed both methods frankly with them and let them make their choice.

Every one of these thirty-seven questions I think of as a *magic phrase,* because they have proved to be truly magic for me in selling.

Now, how can you hit the bull's-eye with these questions if you sell something other than insurance?

Well, of the thirty-seven questions used, *twenty-five are entirely general.* Let me show you what I mean:

Let's assume, for example, you are a hardware salesman calling on retail hardware stores. You have been referred to this prospect by a man you've already sold.

You. Mr. Doyle?

Doyle. Yes.

You. My name is Doak, John Doak, of the Ace Hardware Company. Your friend, Bill Stafford, asked me to stop in and see you the next time I was in your neighborhood. Can you talk for a few minutes now or would you rather I call later? (*As you say this, hand him the card of introduction signed by Bill Stafford.*)

Doyle. Good heavens, man. You're wasting your time! I've been dealing for years with the Samson Manufacturing Company. I've just stocked up and I wouldn't consider buying anything more for some time.

You. Mr. Doyle, would you say that Mr. Stafford is a man of good business judgment?

Doyle. Certainly.

You. Would you say he is the kind of man who would intentionally give you a bad steer?

Doyle. No, I don't believe he would.

You. *Good.* Mr. Stafford wants me to tell you how he secured twenty new customers last month because he began selling a certain new article we are now producing. He wants me to tell you how he did it and he thinks you can do the same thing. Do you have enough confidence in Mr. Stafford's judgment to take ten minutes to find out about this?

Doyle. Yes, of course. Go ahead.

. . . I have used here only the first four questions. You will find it a lot of fun and *highly profitable* to test for yourself all of the questions and see how naturally and effectively *you* can adopt them for whatever you sell.

The Secret of Making Appointments: In "Scene 2" you noticed that Mr. Connor wanted to give me the brush-off by trying to draw me into a discussion. He said, "But boiled down, you are going to try to sell us insurance, isn't that right?" I replied: "Mr. Connor, I want you to distinctly understand that, as a result of our interview this afternoon, you are not going to be asked to buy life insurance. You face a problem and I am going to show you two methods of meeting that problem."

There is the critical moment of the approach!

Regardless of what you are selling, as soon as you indicate that you want to sell something you are licked right there, and the chances of getting an appointment later are ruined. Even to this day, I must be on my guard not to allow myself to be drawn into a sales talk over the phone. I must concentrate on one thing, and one thing alone: selling an *appointment*.

33.

Sharpshooting
for the Right Key Man

ONE FRIDAY MORNING, while lining up my itinerary for the following week, I phoned a friend of mine and found that he was in Florida. Shortly after his return I invited him to have lunch with me.

When I met him, he looked wonderful with his fresh Florida tan and he told me with great enthusiasm all about his trip. He and an old friend of his and their wives had taken their vacation together. I enjoyed hearing all about it. Finally I said, "Jack, tell me more about this friend of yours."

Well, it developed that his friend was sales manager of a very substantial business. Ten years previously, he had been induced to go with this company for only a small increase in salary over what he had been making. However, he was allowed to buy 25 per cent interest in the business at an attractive price and pay for it out of the profits. Now, after ten years, he owned the stock almost clear. Jack told me that Lou was by far the most valuable man in that organization.

I said, "Jack, *there* is a man I would like to talk to." So Jack signed one of my cards of introduction.

The next day, as I handed the card to Jack's friend, I said, "Mr. Bell, do you know this man?"

He read the card with a smile as he saw Jack's signature and asked: "What did you want to see me about?"

"You!" I smiled.

"What about me?" he asked.

"Mr. Bell, I am a life insurance salesman. Jack suggested that I ought to know you. I know you are busy. Can you talk for a few minutes now, or would you rather I call later?"

He then gave me the customary "brush-off" talk. It was impossible for him to buy any more life insurance for the present, and when he did get around to it he had a friend, etc., etc.

I said, "Mr. Bell, after your wonderful vacation with Jack in Florida, I wouldn't want to give you the impression that he told me anything about your private affairs, but in his enthusiasm for the superb job you have done here in this business, Jack asked me to stop and see you the next time I was in your neighborhood. Can you spare five minutes right now?"

"Well, go ahead," he said politely.

I then went right through with my regular "approach talk" and the questions, then said: "Well, my five minutes are up. Is there anything else you would like to tell me?"

"No," he answered, "I think you've got a pretty complete picture there."

As I stood up I said: "Mr. Bell, how did you happen to get into this business?"

He then opened up and told me the whole story and explained the proposition of how his share of the profits had been used to gradually pay for the 25 per cent stock interest he had been buying.

He listened with eager interest as I gave him the usual talk. If anything happened to him, the chances were that his business might never make money again. Immediately upon his death his salary would be discontinued, and his family probably would receive no income from the business. Didn't he think this would be unfair because he had been struggling ten years, and sacrificed a large salary in order to make this investment. . . .

I asked him if he didn't think it would be a fine thing for his company to insure his life so that in the event of his death, his wife and children would be paid off *immediately?*

He agreed to an examination, and after having him approved for $100,000 I interviewed the president, a man seventy-four years old. I said: "It was wise of you to sell this stock to Mr. Bell, but in the event of his death, don't you think it would be *unwise* to let his wife and minor children become the owners of 25 per cent of the stock in this corporation? They *could* cause a lot of trouble. Besides, wouldn't the company need that stock for the development of another good man? Hasn't it been your experience, Mr. President, that the type of man you would want to fill this kind of position is usually well situated? Wouldn't Mr. Bell's stock be a big inducement to the *right* man to leave his present position by offering him an interest in your business?"

The president offered the excuse that with high taxes and cost of labor, the business wasn't in a position to spend any more money on insurance.

"That is the very reason I am presenting this plan," I said. "In fact, it is the *only* reason I am here!"

... After I got a check for $3,487, Lou Bell walked out to the front door with me and I could tell that he was thrilled. He said, "Listen, you don't realize what you've done to get that much money out of him. He is a grand old man, but he's got a balance there in that checkbook that would knock your eye out —yet, you can't get him to pay off a little old mortgage on this building!"

I have found that by singling out the important key man in an organization and building my talk around him, I can frequently make a comparatively easy sale. And usually, it is a substantial sale.

I talk with him individually, pledge him to say nothing to the others, tell him I will take care of that. Usually, on the one side will be the majority stockholder and on the other side, the minority stockholders. Each side has its special interest and I make my appeal accordingly.

Later, I frequently can go back and sell him personally and often other members of the group.

34.

He Wouldn't Talk to Salesmen,
But I Sold Him $137,500

AFTER I THANKED a very successful salesman one day for
his check covering a substantial amount of new business, I
said, "Mr. Williams, do you remember how I happened to meet
you?"

"Yes, Ray Kroll sent you to see me."

"Do you regret that Ray sent me?" I asked with a happy grin.

"Not at all," he admitted.

"You have been successful in selling some of the biggest manufacturers in the city. If one of them happened to walk in here
right now, you wouldn't hesitate to introduce me to him, would
you?" I asked, smiling.

"No, of course not."

"Would you mind giving me the name of one of these men,
and allow me to call on him sometime, using your name just
as I used Ray Kroll's name when I first called on you?"

"Well, I couldn't do that," he said. "You see, I am a salesman.
These people are my customers, and I'm afraid they might not
like it if I sent another salesman to call on them."

"I understand how you feel," I said. "I'll tell you what I'll
do. Give me the name of someone you know, under fifty, who
is making money. I promise you I'll *never* mention your name
to him."

He laughed and said, "Say, listen! Don't mention my name,
but if you can get in to see Henry Krauss, a manufacturer of
knit-goods machinery, Front and Allegheny Avenue, it may be

worth your while. He's a crude, uneducated German, but he's a genius! He's an inventor. Forty-two years old, a wife and three small children. I happen to know he has no insurance. He won't even talk to insurance men."

The next day I dropped in to see Mr. Krauss without an appointment. The girl in the office slid open a tiny window. She said, "Mr. Krauss is busy. Who shall I say wants to see him?"

"Tell him Mr. Bettger is out here. A friend of his told me to stop in for a minute and meet him."

Pretty soon, the dumbest looking face I ever saw on a businessman peered through the small window. I recalled the description of him. It was Krauss all right. It couldn't be anybody else.

ME. Mr. Krauss, a friend of yours asked me to stop in and see you the next time I was in your neighborhood, but he asked me not to mention his name. Can you talk for a few minutes now, or would you rather I call later?

KRAUSS (*with a thick, guttural German accent, which I couldn't possibly imitate here*). Vat did you vunt?

ME. I don't know.

KRAUSS. Vat do you mean? (*He seemed stumped by my answer.*)

ME. Your friend said he thinks I might be able to help you, but I don't know whether I can, unless I can ask you a few questions. May I come in?

KRAUSS. Did you vunt to sell me something?

ME. No. Not today I don't. Later, I may want to help you *buy* something.

KRAUSS. (*He closed the window without a word, and I watched him disappear through a swinging door. I waited several minutes, and was about to leave when the fire-escape door opened and out walked Krauss, dragging his feet. There was absolutely no expression on his face. He looked and acted like a moron. He stopped in front of me and just waited for me to talk.*)

ME. Mr. Krauss, my name is Bettger. I am a life insurance

salesman but I'm not here to sell you anything today. I just wanted to meet you. I can't tell by the color of your eyes, or the color of your hair what your situation is ... (*And I went right through with my regular approach talk. When I came to that part,* "Would you mind if I asked you a few questions?" *he spoke up.*)

KRAUSS. I don't want any insurance. I got a friend in my lodge. I buy insurance from him. (*He spoke such broken-English, I could scarcely understand half his words.*)

ME. How much insurance are you going to buy from your friend?

KRAUSS. No. I buy no insurance.

ME. (*There was an embarrassing pause for nearly a minute. It didn't look possible that this man could have a brain in his head. However, recalling that my friend said he was a genius, I did my best to look at him with an expression of admiration and respect. I thought I'd try one more question.*) Mr. Krauss, how did you happen to get started in this business?

With a little encouragement from time to time, I then heard one of the most amazing and inspiring stories of my entire selling career.

... Born in Germany, he had lost both parents when he was ten years of age. Went to work, and later, when he was old enough, joined the Germany Navy. Finally came to America, got a job in the factory of a manufacturer, and boarded with an older, married sister. At night, he spent most of his time down in the cellar, working on ideas he thought would improve the products and the machinery of the company he worked for. For each invention he worked out, the company "rewarded" him with a dollar a week raise! So he quit them, and started for himself in one room of an unheated old building that hadn't been rented for years. ...

As I listened to his story with excitement and sincere admiration—of how he worked *even now* sixteen, seventeen hours a day—he confided in me that he was *outselling* his old employers!

I was surprised how excited he got as he went on with his story. One banker had refused to lend him three hundred dollars, and now, only a few years later, the same banker had come around to his rapidly expanding plant and wanted to lend him three hundred *thousand* dollars!

"Well," I said, "Mr. Krauss, that is a *wonderful* story! . . . While you were working so hard building this business, did you ever find time to get married?"

"Sure," he smiled for the first time, "and I've got three children."

"Wonderful!" I laughed, with a feeling of genuine happiness for the guy. "I'd like to see them sometime. How old are they?"

Soon he was drawing a diagram on a piece of paper showing me how to get out to his home some evening to meet his family. His wife, he said, had worked for him as bookkeeper and was actually his partner. But when the family started getting too big she stopped coming into the office altogether.

ME. Well, Mr. Krauss, what are your ambitions now? Are you all through growing, or do you plan to keep going and getting bigger?

KRAUSS. I am buying a new building. This place is too small and is unsuited for my plant.

ME. Have you made settlement for the new building yet?

KRAUSS. Not yet.

ME. Are you going to buy the building yourself?

KRAUSS. Well, we are incorporated now, so the company will buy it.

ME. Has your wife got any money?

KRAUSS. No, she's got no money.

ME. I thought you said she was in partnership with you.

KRAUSS. That's right, but the government made me stop paying her a salary.

ME. Did you ever buy her interest in the partnership?

KRAUSS. No.

ME. *Good.* Why don't you pay her what you owe her for her share of the partnership? Then, with that money, let *her* buy the building and be the owner, and the corporation will pay her a good rental. With the rent money she can pay the interest on the mortgage, amortize it, pay fire insurance, all carrying charges, repairs, etc. She can also pay all your living expenses and buy enough insurance on your life to liquidate the mortgage—also pay the inheritance taxes in the event of your death.

I was amazed how fast this "moron" ate up these ideas with only a couple of questions!

I had him examined and approved for the company's limit. I learned later that he did check my ideas with his bank the day after I called on him. And he went through with everything just as I suggested. His wife bought $75,000 of insurance on his life, and assigned it to the bank which took a $75,000 mortgage on the new building.

I went out to his home and spent the evening with him and his attractive wife, arriving early enough to see all three children—two girls and a boy.

A few days later, I phoned and told him I had something I'd like to tell him about; would he have lunch with me?

This was the beginning of a plan which he entered into with the trust department of his bank acting as co-trustees with his wife, and also the most valuable key man in his plant. Some of the company's stock was sold to this key man. The whole plan was wrapped around the ten-year-old son, named after Dad. The idea was for Junior to eventually enter the business with his father. If the father should die, the key man was to teach and train the son, to eventually become head of the business and principal owner.

Under the Deed of Trust, the son was to gradually buy the controlling interest—his mother and sisters to be paid off, through the trustees, out of the profits of the business. Part of that purchase price was protected with $25,000 Ordinary Life, Family Maintenance Rider, Twenty Year Period (totalling $75,000 commuted value). This contract also was applied for, bought and owned by Mrs. Krauss, his wife.

Mr. Krauss took this "father and son" idea so seriously that, during the summer while his family was living at their seashore cottage, he frequently brought his boy up to the city with him on Monday mornings, and the two of them worked at the plant three or four days, returning to the seashore usually on Thursday.

. . . Well, this whole plan turned out to be a wise thing for everybody concerned. Only a few short years later, Mr. Krauss died suddenly, before Junior finished high school. Everything has worked out successfully right on schedule, just as we planned it.

To the inexperienced life underwriter, this case may sound like an unusual, isolated experience—but it is not. It is a sound, practical plan that I have seen work out successfully so frequently in corporations, partnerships, and proprietorships, large and small, that it became a routine part of my business and one of the most exciting and satisfying. Yet, one of the most productive.

That is why I have devoted an entire section of this book to the methods I learned and used to help businessmen plan for the protection and perpetuation of their businesses.

ANALYSIS OF THE BASIC PRINCIPLES
IN THIS SALE

1. This experience taught me once again that it is always safest and best to *overestimate*—never underestimate a man.

2. Most of us need inspiration. My greatest inspiration has come, not from *great* men, but from ordinary men like myself. Listening in on their lives— how they overcame handicaps and mistakes—has inspired me. Most of these men, I found, had periods of great discouragement and despair, were

tempted to quit, just as I so often was. How they solved their problems and finally came out victorious has never failed to give me a great lift; has helped restore my courage and faith. I find myself saying, "If he can do it, *I* can do it!"

3. One of the most motivating parts of this Krauss sale, as it is in most of these cases, was this: When I drew a parallel between his own experience with his former employers, he wanted to do something for his most valuable key man; something more definite and substantial than a "dollar a week raise"!

Credit Herschel C. Logan

"Partnerships often finish in quarrels; but I was happy in this, that mine were all carried on and ended amicably owing, I think, a good deal to the precaution of having very explicitly, settled in our Articles, everything to be done by, or expected from, each partner, so there was nothing to dispute, which precaution I would therefore recommend to all who enter into partnerships."

BENJAMIN FRANKLIN

HOW I CONQUERED FEAR AND DEVELOPED COURAGE AND SELF-CONFIDENCE RAPIDLY

I believe one of the biggest problems for most of us is how to develop courage and self-confidence. At twenty-nine years of age, I found myself a complete failure as a salesman. I was unable to get a job of any kind. I became so unnerved, I couldn't even go out and *ask* for a job. I had such a yellow streak, I was ashamed to tell my own wife about it.

I knew I had to find a way to do something about it—and quick! In desperation, I joined one of Dale Carnegie's courses in Public Speaking. At first, I was so terrified I didn't see how I could possibly go through with it. But somehow I did. And it proved to be a turning point in my life! In fact, it would be almost impossible for me to exaggerate how important this training was to my career.

It helped me develop courage and self-confidence rapidly! It broadened my vision, stimulated my enthusiasm, and helped me express my ideas more convincingly to other men.

It helped me destroy the biggest enemy I ever had to face—*fear!*

This may read like a "commercial" for the Dale Carnegie course. But it is not. My present purpose is merely to relate facts. I try never to lose an opportunity to express my appreciation and gratitude for what the Dale Carnegie course has meant to me.

I would urge any man or woman who is being held back by fear, and who lacks courage and self-confidence, to join the best Public Speaking course in his or her community. Don't just join *any* lecture course. Join only a course where you make a talk at every meeting, because that's what you want—experience in speaking.

If you can't find a good, practical course, do as Ben Franklin did. Ben recognized the value of such training and he formed the "Junto" right here in my home town. Meet one night each week. Appoint a new chairman to serve each week or month. If you can't get a good instructor, criticize each other, as the Junto did two hundred years ago.

Franklin, in his later years, wrote about the Junto speaking experiences as one of the most important things he had ever done.

PART SIX

Why Should You
Do Something for Nothing?

35.

This Job Cost Me More Time and Energy Than I Calculated

TWO MEN from the Y.M.C.A. approached the president of the Life Underwriters' Association in Philadelphia about getting the Association to sponsor a practical course in life insurance salesmanship. It was to be given under the direction of the Central "Y" Branch, 1421 Arch Street. The course to be taught, however, by a large personal producer.

Such a school was already being conducted in New York City, the first of its kind ever attempted in the country. And, they said, it was proving to be very successful.

The president told the "Y" representatives that the idea appealed to him very much if they could induce a successful life insurance salesman to tackle the job of teaching such a school. He instructed them to take the matter up with the Association's Educational Chairman. At the time, that happened to be me.

When they presented their plan, I became enthusiastic about the idea and promised to recommend it to the Board of Directors at our next meeting.

Well, the Board was unanimously in favor of such a course, but seemed to feel that it would be impossible to find a substantial personal producer who would be willing to give enough time to such an undertaking. It would mean two nights a week, plus a lot of time for preparation. It was sure to result in a big loss of production and money to him.

Somebody spoke up and said, "Mr. President, I move that

our Association sponsor the plan, and I nominate Frank Bettger to be the teacher of the class!"

"I second that motion!" quickly called out another director.

"All in favor of that motion say Aye," said the president.

"*Aye!*" was the unanimous vote . . . except mine.

"*Wait a minute!*" I got up and protested, "*But I couldn't . . .*"

My voice was drowned out by loud talk and applause. The president's gavel hit the table with a bang. "Frank Bettger has been *unanimously* elected!" he grinned.

Naturally, I could have absolutely refused to serve. But here's what happened: 107 men and women representing twenty-six different life insurance companies enrolled. Many of them had been selling insurance from ten to twenty years. Some had just started and several were only considering going into the business.

We held forty sessions during the winter. Tuesday evenings, we devoted entirely to selling. Thursday evenings, to the fundamentals of life insurance.

Teaching that school cost me even more time and energy than I calculated. My production fell off. At the time it seemed like a great burden. But looking back later, this was the real picture:

1. During the winter, I became good friends with Robert P. Koehler, Assistant Educational Director of the Central "Y." Sitting in on parts of our early classes, Mr. Koehler seemed to become worried over the fact that he was ridiculously under-insured. I found time to relieve him of part of that worry by insuring him for $10,000.

2. Mr. Koehler later referred me to a friend of his, forty-two years of age with a young wife and three small children—but no insurance! His name was Gustav Weber. I was astonished when I got into his situation with him, that he had suddenly loomed up as the *second largest* builder of homes in the city! Over a period of fifteen months, I insured Mr. Weber for $350,000, premiums amounting to $11,900 annually.

3. However, within less than three years, through a series

of incredibly unfortunate circumstances, Gustav Weber went broke and was forced to go through bankruptcy. All his life insurance was about to lapse. His creditors joined together and retained a lawyer to protect their interests. His name was Nelson West, located in the Stock Exchange Building, 1411 Walnut Street, Philadelphia. I went to see Mr. West and asked him if he would be interested in an idea that might help the creditors reduce their losses. Naturally, he wanted to know how. I said I had handled all of Mr. Weber's insurance—over $300,-000. There were values in these polices; would he give me five minutes at the next creditors' meeting?

"Be here in my office Saturday morning, 10:30, and I'll see that you get five minutes," he agreed.

Their meeting had been called for ten o'clock, so I arrived at 10:15 and asked the receptionist to let Mr. West know that Mr. Bettger was there. In a few minutes I was told to go into Mr. West's office. Eight creditors were seated around facing the lawyer's desk. Mr. West said: "Gentlemen, this is Mr. Bettger, Mr. Weber's insurance man. I agreed to give Mr. Bettger five minutes this morning to present an idea he says may help to reduce your losses on Mr. Weber."

I wasn't asked to sit down, so standing, I said:

"Gentlemen, I have $350,000 of insurance on Mr. Weber's life. He has paid two annual premiums. He is unable to continue this insurance and it will all lapse within the next thirty days. Mr. Weber seems anxious to co-operate in any way he can to minimize your losses and he has consented to execute absolute assignments of these policies over to you. If you pay *one* year's premium, at the end of the year you may surrender your policies and receive back every dollar you paid, plus about 30 per cent profit. If Mr. Weber should die in the meantime, you will receive the full face amount of these policies outright, which would wipe out your losses entirely. I don't know whether you know it, but at the present time, Mr. Weber is uninsurable. No company would take a dollar of insurance on his life. He lost about twenty-five pounds during the last two months, and appears to be a really sick man.

"At the end of the year, if you want to continue this insurance, or any part of it, you may do so. Simply pay another year's premium. At the end of the following year, if you should cash your policy in, you will still get back *more money* than you paid."

One man spoke up: "How much would $100,000 cost to carry it for one year?"

"$3,000," I answered.

"If I should take $100,000, what protection would I have? In other words, if I wanted to surrender my policy for cash at any time, would I have to get Mr. Weber's consent or signature?"

"No, sir. Once he executes an absolute assignment to you, it becomes *your* property to do with as you please—regardless of whether Mr. Weber lives or dies."

"I'll take $100,000," said Henry R. Strathmann (builder's supply business), who had been asking the questions.

"We'll take $100,000," spoke up Mr. Brown, Treasurer of the Hajoca Corporation.

. . . Within five minutes those creditors had agreed to take $300,000 of that insurance.

This meeting of Gustav Weber's creditors was only the beginning of an amazing chain of events that opened up a wide circle of new friends and clients for me. In the next chapter I want to tell you about one of them, because it taught me a lesson that I had never realized was so important in selling and dealing with people.

So what seemed in the beginning like a thankless job at the Y.M.C.A., which was going to cost me a lot of time and money, turned out to be a blessing in disguise. It not only led indirectly to one of the handsomest paying activities I ever became interested in, but something else happened to me that year which was far more important than any financial profit: The responsibility of teaching that class of 107 men and women made it compulsory for me to study and prepare. It forced me to put into practical use the training I had taken in the Dale

Carnegie Public Speaking course. These experiences made it possible, later, for me to accept the superintendency of a Sunday School, which office I continued for nine years. Those things combined proved to be the most important turning point of my life. It taught me that *it is more blessed to give than to receive.*

I have tried both ways: "Go-getter" and "Go-giver." I found what thousands of others have found: being a "go-giver" is a new way of life. It gave me a new enthusiasm, an enthusiasm that helped me overcome fear, become more successful in business, make more money and enjoy a healthier, richer and happier life.

36.

"The Hell with It!"

I MANAGED TO GET a letter of introduction from one of Gustav Weber's creditors to Edward A. Schmidt, wealthy banker and brewer. Not long before this I wouldn't have even *thought* of trying to sell a man as big as Mr. Schmidt. He had built up the Schmidt Brewery to the largest in Philadelphia. And Philadelphia is the second largest brewery city in America.

Yet, Mr. Schmidt devoted only *half* his time to this job. Mornings, he was president of the Northwestern National Bank and Trust Company.

He was widely known as a marvelous organizer.

When I met him, I was amazed to find he was sixty-nine years old. But in perfect health, with the alertness and appearance of a man of fifty. I quickly learned why so few salesmen attempted to interview him.

As I was ushered into his private office, he stood up, looking so stern that it scared me. It looked like a knockout in the first round. In addition to that, he had devised a unique technique calculated to knock salesmen out in the *first ten seconds!* Let me tell you what it was:

I handed him my letter of introduction. He read two sentences. As he was reading: "In my opinion, Frank Bettger is one of the best qualified life insurance men in Philadelphia," Mr. Schmidt turned his back on me, pressed a button, and I almost fell on the floor when I saw foot-high neon letters light up a brilliant red, directly over his head:

THE HELL WITH IT!

I then did something without realizing it, which might have been the *only* thing that saved me from a quick knockout! I broke into a laugh that I could hardly control, and kept on laughing so hard and so long that finally that stern face of his softened up just a little, and I noticed a slight twinkle in his eyes.

Then I said: "Mr. Schmidt, I realize how busy you are. May I have the courtesy of five minutes of your valuable time—by my watch?"

I gave him the usual opening talk in less than a minute, then was able to obtain the information I needed about his financial affairs . . . more than he had ever given anybody else, so he told me.

That information enabled me to present facts to Mr. Schmidt later, which showed him the serious difficulty his estate would undergo, in the event of his death, to raise enough liquid funds to meet the heavy inheritance taxes. I showed him that life insurance provided the *only* solution—if he could get it.

He agreed to co-operate with me on examinations, chest pictures, electro-cardiograms, etc. And finally, five companies issued their limit of insurance on a man of his age. This all took quite a bit of time.

After I received all the policies, I called Mr. Schmidt at the bank for an appointment. He agreed but when I walked into his office with a big smile, he looked as cold as stone. I knew something was wrong. I was afraid he was going to flash that neon sign again. I sat down without a word and just looked at him. "Mr. Bettger," he said, *"I'm not going to take that insurance!"*

I never was more completely dumbfounded in my life. Finally, I managed to say, *"Why?"*

"Because," he declared, *"I'm not going to take it!"*

There was a sickly silence as I dropped my head, looked down and waited. But that, apparently was *all*. There was great tension in the air.

When I looked up right into his face, he was glaring at me as though I had committed some great wrong against him. I said, "Mr. Schmidt, you are one of the most successful men in Philadelphia. I know you must have a good reason why you've decided not to take this insurance. Would you mind telling me what it is?"

He hesitated. So I added: "If your reason is sound, there's nothing I can say that will change it. On the other hand, if I could suggest another solution, you'll be glad you told me, isn't that right?"

"I haven't got the money to pay for it," was his surprising statement.

"When will you have the money?" I frankly asked.

"Not for four or five months," he replied.

"That's easy," I smiled, "I'll take your note."

"You won't take *my* note," he practically sneered.

"Why not?" I asked, as though this would only be routine business.

"What would you do with the note?" he asked.

"Discount it and pay the insurance companies," I said.

"And every bank in Philadelphia would say, 'Edward A. Schmidt is paying his insurance premiums with notes,'" said he.

"I'll discount the note in New York," I promised.

"And two days later, that note would be back in Philadelphia. No, I've never given anybody my note in my life, and I'm not going to start now," he declared.

I could see the interview was over.

I returned to my office *sick*. I wouldn't be good for anything the rest of the day. It was a *lot* of money. After those policies had been issued, and I got them in my hands, I allowed myself to start figuring how much I was going to get out of the sale. I even began figuring how I was going to use that money. Always a foolish thing to do.

There I sat in a daze. "What should I have said to him?" I asked myself. "What else *could* I have said to him?" There must be *something*.

I began to think the whole thing through from every angle. . . . Suddenly an idea hit me! I grabbed the phone and called Mr. Schmidt.

"I've got the answer!" I shouted in his ear with excitement.

"What do you mean, *'you've got the answer,'* " Mr. Schmidt asked coldly.

"I've got the *right answer!*" I repeated excitedly. "May I come right up?"

"I can't imagine what you mean, 'You've got the right answer.' . . . How long will it take?"

"It won't take me twenty seconds. I'll be in your office in ten minutes," I assured him confidently.

"Well," he said reluctantly, "I'm leaving here at twelve o'clock, so you'd better hurry."

Ten minutes later when I walked into his office he looked at me with the coldest banker's eye I ever saw. "Well, what's this idea you've got?" he asked impatiently.

I sat down directly in front of him, looked him straight in the eye and said, "You discount *my* note."

"Say that again," he said, surprised.

"Let your bank discount *my* note, and *I'll* pay the insurance companies."

"And then what?" he asked.

"When you are ready, you pay me the amount of the note and I'll repay the bank."

"Do you have an account here at our bank?"

"No, but I can open one right now," I smiled.

There was complete silence for several seconds. I watched him quietly as he thought.

"What will you have to show that I owe you this money?" he asked.

"Nothing," I answered.

"Suppose I should happen to die before I'm ready to pay?"

"I would deliver checks from the insurance companies for the full amount of the policies to your executors. I'm sure I wouldn't have much trouble collecting the amount of my note from your executors."

"Suppose *you* should die?" he asked.

"That is the *only* chance I am taking," I admitted. "I feel confident, Mr. Schmidt, that if that should happen, you wouldn't see my widow lose that money."

The president of the bank pushed a button. A clerk came in. "Send Mr. Batten here immediately," Mr. Schmidt ordered.

Mr. Batten proved to be the trust officer of the bank. I was introduced to him. "Mr. Bettger wishes to open a checking account. Bring the papers and also a note. We are discounting a note for him."

Four months later, Mr. Schmidt paid me in full and I paid my note off at the bank. In addition, he became one of my best centers of influence. And, by the way, if hard work would kill a man, he would have died at a young age. But Edward A. Schmidt lived until he was eighty-four and was alert and active right up till a few weeks before his death.

HOW I ARRIVED AT THE SOLUTION OF THIS CASE

I was inspired one time when I heard Russell Conwell, in his lecture, "Acres of Diamonds," say: "Whatever you have to do at all, put your whole mind into it and hold it there until that is all done. This principle can be adopted by nearly all. . . . This principle makes men great almost anywhere."

I tried to do this, but for a long while it didn't seem to help me. In the final chapter, I am going to tell about a method I learned later that taught me *how to think things through to the final solution.*

37.

"Bread Cast Upon the Waters..."

T HE SHORTEST DAY of the year for me is the day before Christmas. No matter how carefully I plan ahead, when Christmas Eve arrives, I suddenly think of a dozen things I've forgotten! I was having one of those days a few weeks after the creditors' meeting in Nelson West's office, when it occurred to me that I had overlooked Miss Sara Graham, then the head switchboard operator at the Fidelity Mutual's head office.

I immediately called and asked how long she was going to be there. Well, it was almost noon and she was getting ready to leave for the day and do some last minute shopping.

I said, "I've got an envelope I intended to deliver to you in person, but . . ."

"Oh, Mr. Bettger," Miss Graham said earnestly, "please think nothing of it. You shouldn't do that anyhow. You know the company pays me for whatever I do for you, and I really don't expect anything."

Well, Christmas was the only time of the year I could show my appreciation for the extra effort she always made to locate me promptly and see that I received messages that might be important.

Finally, she admitted that she would be stopping at a Mr. Fox's office in midtown at two o'clock. I went out of my way and missed lunch, just for the satisfaction it gave me to hand her personally a Christmas envelope, containing a modest token of my appreciation for her many kind and courteous favors.

Then, I realized that I was getting pretty hungry. The Penn A.C. was only a block away, so I dropped in for a quick bite.

As I walked into the cafeteria I saw my new friend from the creditors' meeting, Henry R. Strathmann, sitting alone, eating lunch.

I stopped, and with a bright smile said, "Merry Christmas, Mr. Strathmann."

"Oh, hello, Mr. Bettger," he answered, seeming agreeably surprised to find I was a Penn A.C. member. "Are you all alone?"

"Yes, I am."

"After you get your tray, come over and sit here," he invited.

"You bet," I agreed.

When I came back with my tray I said, "What are you doing in town so late today—Christmas shopping?"

"No. You may be surprised. I just came from the bank. *I have just completed arrangements for the biggest deal I ever made in my life!*"

I think he was *bursting* to tell the first *friend* he saw!

"Sounds very exciting!" I said with great interest. "I'd love to hear all about it."

And then he launched right into a fascinating story about a deal that would make him probably the largest individual builder's supply operator in the East! Naturally, it involved quite a large loan at the bank.

I said, "Mr. Strathmann, would you mind if I ask you a personal question?"

"Not at all. What is it?"

"In making this loan at the bank, I suppose you had to put up some collateral, didn't you?"

"Yes," he answered without hesitating. "I covered the entire loan with my own bonds which I took out of my safe-deposit box this morning."

Then he told me the amount of the loan! It was a big one all right—and every cent of it covered by *his own* bonds!

I looked at him in dead earnest and said: "Mr. Strathmann, do you know what you are telling me? You are telling me that you need X dollars of life insurance!"

He looked me straight in the eye, and I looked back at him

steadily without blinking an eyelash. It seemed like almost a minute that we just sat there staring at each other with not a word spoken.

"Why?" he asked, finally.

He knew the answer as well as I did, but he was just stalling for time.

"If anything should happen to you, while your good bonds are assigned to the bank, wouldn't they sell them on the market in order to liquidate your loan?"

"Yes, I believe that is right," he agreed.

"Wouldn't this be a tremendous loss to your estate?"

"Yes, it would," agreed Mr. Strathmann.

"Wouldn't this be a *happier* Christmas for you if you made up your mind today to protect your loan with life insurance, knowing that if anything does happen to you, your bonds would be returned to your family free and clear of your indebtedness?"

"You're right," admitted Mr. Strathmann.

"You look as though you never felt better in your life. Let's get the examination made as soon as possible, and after the policies are issued, we can take them over to your bank and assign them as additional collateral," I suggested.

... You've heard that expression "Bread cast upon the waters sometimes comes back strawberry shortcake"! Well, I believe in that principle literally. Only I never saw it happen so fast before!

The Strathmann sale was one of the largest, quickest, yet one of the easiest sales I have ever made. But I never would have had this "lucky break" if I hadn't gone out of my way and made the extra effort on Christmas Eve to show my appreciation to Sara Graham.

And I never would have met Henry Strathmann in the first place if I hadn't insured Gustav Weber. In fact I wouldn't have met Gustav Weber if I hadn't insured Robert Koehler. But then I never would have met Robert Koehler *if I hadn't taught the class at the Y.M.C.A.!*

And this was only the beginning! I find it impossible to trace back the endless chain of leads and sales that had their beginning in that class on salesmanship at the Y.M.C.A.

Yet *none* of it would have happened if I had considered the job from the money angle. From *that* angle I couldn't afford it. The job paid me only $250 for the entire season—five months out of the year. . . .

Although I had given so much time to the Y.M.C.A. course, not long afterward I received the following letter:

Dear Mr. Bettger:

We have been pleased to note that as a result of the business which you have placed in our company, you have been listed among the first ten leading special agents and brokers of our entire national organization. We realize that your own company has first call upon your business, and we appreciate that part of it which you have found possible to submit to the Prudential. I did not want to pass up the opportunity of commending you upon your standing.

Please accept my hearty congratulations and best wishes that during the years ahead your efforts will be rewarded with even greater success.

Yours very truly,

Arthur L. Stephans,
Supervisor

THE DOLLARS AND CENTS VALUE
OF A CALL

My good friend, Lester H. Shingle, President of the Single Leather Company, Camden, N. J., one of the largest manufacturers of leather in their line, said to me one day: "Frank, do you know you said something to me one day that helped me go out the following day and make a sale; and that sale led to others that amounted to thousands of dollars?"

"Really? That sounds exciting. Tell me all about it," I urged.

"You came into my office one day and tried to sell me some life insurance. Well, you failed to make the sale, but as you got up to leave, I said, 'Frank, I'm sorry this call has not meant something to you.'

" 'It has,' you smiled. 'The fact is, I just made eighteen dollars while I was talking with you.'

" 'That's fine,' I said. 'It has been painless to me. How do you figure it?'

"You said, 'Because I keep records of all the calls I make, and I find on the average every call is worth eighteen dollars. So I never worry whether I sell a man or not. I know if I keep seeing 'em, old man law of averages will take care of me!'

"Well," continued Lester, "next day I attended a funeral service. After the service, it was too late to get back to my office, but remembering what you had said about every call netting you eighteen dollars, I decided to try it out for myself, as we had a customer in that neighborhood.

"When I got there, as so often is the case, the Purchasing Agent said, 'Sorry, we are not in the market just now for anything in your line.'

"When I got up to go, I grinned at him and said,

'Thank you just the same, Mr. Jones. I have made eighteen dollars by calling on you.'

"Jones looked at me in surprise. 'What do you mean?' he asked.

"Then I told him the interesting story you had told me, how you kept a record of all your calls and discovered that on the *average*, every call made was worth eighteen dollars.

" 'Wait a minute,' laughed Jones. 'Your call ought to be worth as much as an insurance salesman's. Do you by any chance have X type of leather?'

"Now this was something we had not been selling them, and if I hadn't made that call, we would not have received an inquiry for it.

"The profit on that order was worth more than ten times eighteen dollars, but if I hadn't been reminded after the funeral of what you told me the day before, I would not have made that call."

PART SEVEN

If You Were My Own Brother...

38.

From Bankrupt to Million Dollar Producer Within One Year

ONE MORNING IN JANUARY, last year, I was in a general agent's office placing part of a line of business on an overage case. I asked about his largest producer, a friend of mine whom we'll call Bill Jones. I was surprised when this general agent said: "Bill just finished his worst year since he came into the business fourteen years ago.

"I'm really worried about him, Frank," he said. "I've never seen Bill in such a state of mind. He refuses to attend our meetings—won't talk to anybody—says he just wants to be left alone. He told his wife that if she didn't stop spending money, he was going to lay right down in the middle of the road ... and that's just what he *is* doing now."

I said, "Would you mind if I had a talk with Bill?"

"Frank," he said, "if there is anybody Bill might listen to, it would be you."

First, I had the general agent get out Bill's records. I could hardly believe what I saw. . . .

Luck was with me. Bill was in his office, all alone. I knew Bill well. So when I walked in, I closed the door after me. It had been years since I'd been in his office. Naturally, he was taken by surprise. I sat down and looked at him. I was shocked! He looked like a mental case.

He wouldn't look at me.

"What's the matter, Bill?" I asked.

BILL. What do you mean?
ME. What are you worried about?
BILL. (*No answer.*)

ME. You're scared! What are you afraid of?

BILL (*looking at me for the first time*). There's nothing wrong with me that money wouldn't cure.

ME. In addition to that, Bill, isn't there something else? Listen, Bill, you can talk plain with me. Tell me *anything*.

BILL. No, that's the only thing. I don't know what's happened to me—my business. It's got on my nerves. *I can't pay my bills!*

ME. Would $25,000 help you?

BILL. Are you kidding?

ME. No, I'm not kidding. I'm going to give you $25,000.

I pulled my chair over, alongside of him. "*Here's all you do!*" I began putting down some figures, drawing steps. I showed him what was happening to him. . . .

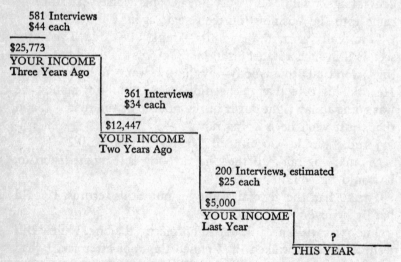

581 Interviews
$44 each

$25,773
YOUR INCOME
Three Years Ago

361 Interviews
$34 each

$12,447
YOUR INCOME
Two Years Ago

200 Interviews, estimated
$25 each

$5,000
YOUR INCOME
Last Year

?
THIS YEAR

Bill just sat there quietly, but intensely interested, while I finished making the diagram.

"There it is, Bill," I said. "It's just that simple! I know what you've been going through. I've been all through it *myself*. You feel like a ballplayer in a bad slump. You feel as though you couldn't even *buy* a hit. There's *nothing* wrong with you! You're no different today, Bill. You are just as good as you were three years ago—*better!* You are a *great* salesman—one of the *best!* . . . See that $25,000 at the top of these steps? *It's yours! You're going back up there this year!"*

I stood up. Bill jumped up and grabbed my hand. "Frank," he said with emotion, "this is the greatest thing that has ever happened to me in my life. I don't know how to thank you for coming in." Tears were welling in his eyes.

"No, it's no good, Bill . . . I'm not leaving," I said, as I took off my coat. "You know *what* to do, but let's make sure you know *how* to do it."

. . . We spent four hours getting organized for his next week's work. Bill got so excited he wouldn't go out for lunch, sent a girl out for a couple of sandwiches and coffee.

Before I left there that day, Bill was prepared as he had never been prepared before. He had seven appointments and two luncheon engagements which he arranged over the phone. We planned thirty-six calls for the coming week, in their proper order for each day. He agreed to get a minimum of eight completed questionnaires in order to assure him at least eight closing interviews for the following week. We prepared proposals and Personal Estate Analyses based on discussions we had about appointments he made. In addition to that, Bill pledged to have an absolute minimum of 720 interviews (firsts and finals) for the balance of the year.

When I left there, Bill *knew* he was going to be up there again at the top of those steps—*that year!* As our preparation for the next week kept building up, all he could say was: "This is terrific! *Fantastic!"*

As I shook hands with him to go, he broke down and wept.

The last thing I said to him was this: "Bill, there's only *one* thing that can stop you now. Only *one* thing."

"What's that?" he asked.

"*You!* Everything fails if you skip *one* Self-Organization Day. *Everything! . . .* Which day is going to be your Self-Organization Day?"

"What would you suggest?" he asked.

"Why don't you try Fridays for awhile and see how it works out?" I suggested.

. . . What happened to Bill Jones? Let's look at the record:

One Year Later
549 Interviews
82 Sales
$1,412,000 paid-for Business

And Bill had made $27,078!

Bill Jones, like so many veterans in the business, thought he had "got beyond the time for keeping records."

Clay Hamlin, who raised himself from failure to one of America's greatest salesmen, *failed three times* before he began "definitizing" his work and analyzing his records. Speaking from his own experience and the experience of training many salesmen, Clay puts it this way:

"Substitute anything for selling exposure and you are lost! You will begin to disintegrate and gradually go to pieces. Despondency is largely the product of idleness. Vigorous activity dispels gloom and keeps a man youthful, daring and prosperous!"

One of the prize excuses some salesmen give for not keeping records is "I haven't time!" One salesman asked Richard W. Campbell, life member of the "Million Dollar Round Table," who has produced over a million for twelve consecutive years: "Dick, you are a big producer. How in the world do you ever find time to keep records?"

Dick is a very modest person. Here was his reply: "If it is true that I am a big producer, it is *because* I keep records. If I am doing anything wrong, my records tell me. It is the very reason I am able to avoid slumps and keep my production at a high level."

Before Dick Campbell began keeping records, he became so discouraged he seriously considered leaving Altoona, Pa., for greener pastures. He had about concluded that success was a matter of geography. After he began "definitizing" his work, Dick found Altoona a veritable "Acres of Diamonds."

39.

If You Were My Own Brother,
I Would Say to You What
I'm Going to Say to You Now

IN THE BEGINNING of the book, you remember, I told about going back to the office one Saturday afternoon and having it out with myself. Nobody could get much lower in spirit and more discouraged than I was—couldn't pay my bills—badly in debt to my company.

That was the day I got the vision of a plan of *action!* At first, I thought of it as just a *work sheet;* planning my entire week ahead; a plan to end my confusion.

Important as that was, only a few weeks later, something else happened to me that was of even greater importance: I picked up a book that had a profound effect on my life—*The Autobiography of Benjamin Franklin.* When Franklin was a small printer in Philadelphia and badly in debt, he discovered an idea. A half century later he wrote that to this idea *he owed all his success and happiness.* The idea was simply this:

He chose thirteen subjects which he felt were necessary or desirable for him to acquire and try to master, and he gave a week's strict attention to each subject successively. In this way, he was able to go through his entire list in thirteen weeks, and repeat the process four times a year. "Well," I thought, "if a genius like Benjamin Franklin, one of the wisest and most practical men who ever walked this earth, believed this was the most important thing he ever did, why shouldn't I try it?"

I followed his plan exactly as he told how he used it. I just took it and embodied it in my "13 Weeks' Self-Organizer" which you will find immediately following the close of the book. Each week, you will see one of my principles with a short precept, which fully expresses the extent I gave to its meaning. The first principle is ENTHUSIASM. First thing in the morning and at odd moments during the day, I read the precept on enthusiasm. Just for that one week, I determined each day to double the amount of enthusiasm that I had been putting into my selling and into my life. The second week is SELF-ORGANIZA- TION. And so on, each week. It was the track I ran on!

At the end of one year, I had completed four courses. I found myself doing things naturally and unconsciously that I wouldn't have attempted a year before. Although I fell far short of mastering any of these principles, I found this simple plan a truly magic formula. Without it, I never could have maintained my enthusiasm and, I believe, if a man can maintain enthusiasm long enough, it will produce anything!

Two years after I started using it, I had a big surprise. I received an invitation to speak at the regular monthly luncheon of the Philadelphia Life Underwriters' Association!

I must have read that invitation over a dozen times! I carried it around in my pocket until it became almost too soiled to read.

Yet, only a little more than two years before, I had given up all hope of ever being able to sell insurance, or sell anything. I had *quit!* It just seemed incredible that now, only two years later, I was going to make a speech before the Life Under- writers. . . .

Shortly after I accepted the invitation, I had a big shock. One of the ablest and most respected agency managers in the city phoned Louis Paret, president of the Association, and told him it would be a horrible mistake to have anyone like Bettger for the speaker at an Association meeting. He said he understood that Bettger was a crude, uneducated, broken-down *old* ball- player; never had any business training, and only a short ex- perience selling. Having a man like that, he felt, would lower the standards of the Association, and, if Paret went through with it, none of his men would attend the meeting!

When I heard this, I called Mr. Paret and told him I thought this manager was probably right, and I offered willingly to withdraw and promised him I would not be offended. I said, "Maybe it would be better to wait another year or two."

However, the meeting was held, and I spoke.

I called my subject "The Dollars and Cents Value of a Call." I was astonished how enthusiastically the talk was received by some of the seasoned underwriters. The leading producer of the agency, whose manager had instructed his men not to attend, came "just for the fun of it," he said. But he was the *first* man to shake hands with me after I finished my talk.

Louis Paret invited me to deliver the same talk at the Provident Mutual Life Insurance Company meeting to be held two months later at the company's head office in Philadelphia. At that meeting, I was introduced as "the first outside insurance salesman ever invited to address a Provident Convention."

I was so overwhelmed, it was all I could do to control my emotions and go on with the talk.

The Agency Manager who objected to me as a speaker soon became one of my good friends and best boosters. I never held it against him for objecting to me. I could understand why he felt as he did. It had been such a short time before that I was exactly what he said I was. I could hardly believe the change myself!

Years later, I was astounded to read that John Dewey, regarded as the patron saint of American education, said he would quickly exchange four years of college for a burning interest in something. I realized then that no college in the world can do anything whatever for you except to help you help yourself.

Dale Carnegie, one of America's leaders in adult education, recently said to me: "Frank, it is quite probable that you gave yourself a more practical education by forcing yourself to adopt Benjamin Franklin's 13 Weeks' Plan together with your Self-Organizer, than many men obtain by spending four years in college."

I have tried to write nothing in this book except fundamental principles, principles that *never* change. I have written the book primarily for the life insurance business—the business that took me in, willingly, with open arms, when I was down and out and nobody else wanted me.

Most of these ideas, I hope, will be helpful to salesmen regardless of whether they are selling insurance, or "shoes or ships or sealing wax."

I couldn't go to my grave without telling my story. I had to take the time to write about some of the things that great men gave to me that I have wanted to give to you, instead of letting them die with me. . . .

I know my old partner, Clayt Hunsicker, would have wanted it that way.

FRANK BETTGER'S

13 WEEKS' SELF-ORGANIZER

Name ———————————————————

Address ———————————————————

Company ———————————————————

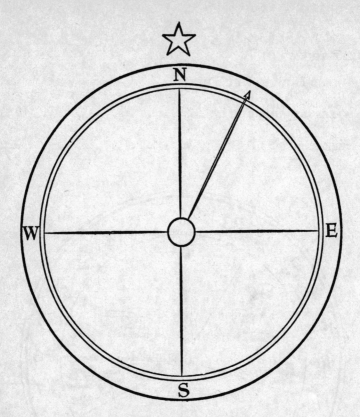

There are five points to a compass:
North, East, South, West
and where you are *now*.

This planner gives you the Facts: where you are now; where you are going; and how to get there.

Carry it with you always. Enter records and facts during the day. Each week, on "Self-Organization Day," total all figures, summarize results for week and year to date. Do this year after year, and you will find yourself enjoying the most exciting and satisfying business in the world—Selling!

If you want to know whether you are going to be a success in selling, the test is easy: Can you organize and control your time?

If not, drop out, for you will surely fail. You may not think so, but you will fail as surely as you live!

Selling can never be reduced to an exact science any more than medicine can be an exact science. However, it is amazing how sales can be measured and forecast by studying the records of salesmen.

Show me any man of ordinary ability who will earnestly follow through the system in this book and I will show you a man who just can't help making good! Yes, you can *insure* a happy and successful career in the greatest business ever devised by man—selling!

Enthusiastically *yours!*

Frank Bettger

YOUR PRODUCTION INSURANCE

( ) Calls
( ) Selling Interviews (Attempts to Close)
( ) *New and Referred Names* (Qualified Prospects)
( ) per cent of Interviews on *New* Prospects

RESULTS: ( ) Closing Interviews Weekly
x48 Weeks
( ) Closing Interviews a year will
produce from ( ) to ( )
Sales a year.

SELF-ORGANIZATION DAY

(Your most important work of the week)

Office—8 A.M.

1. Complete all records to date.
   Review totals. Check yourself to see if you are doing the things you *resolved* you would do to achieve your objectives.

2. Plan MASTER SCHEDULE for next week.

3. Case preparation; Proposals for next week's closing interviews. Concentrate on each interview for appropriate motivating stories, appeals in prospects' language to motivate *action!*

4. Telephone for appointments. Try to arrange ( ) closing appointments a week.

5. Answer all correspondence; other office details.

6. *Resolution* for the week.

7. Meditation period. Prayer.

INVENTORY
OF PROSPECTS
Salable Within 60 Days

Records reveal surprising differences in sources of sales and numbers of calls required to close them. In one industry, 68% of sales come from *new* prospects —and on the first interviews! In another industry, 80% of sales come from *old* prospects—and after the fifth interview! Watch these percentages in *your* records. Then plan each week's list accordingly.

PROSPECTS

	Name	Amount	
		New	*Old*
1		$	$
2			
3			
4			
5			
6			
7			
8			
9			
10			
11			
12			
13			
14			
TOTAL EXPECT TO CLOSE		$	$

PROSPECTS

Name	Amount	
	New	Old
15	$	$
16		
17		
18		
19		
20		
21		
22		
23		
24		
25		
26		
27		
28		
29		
30		
31		
32		
33		
34		
35		
TOTAL	$	$
EXPECT TO CLOSE		

PROSPECTS

Name	Amount	
	New	Old
36	$	$
37		
38		
39		
40		
41		
42		
43		
44		
45		
46		
47		
48		
49		
50		
51		
52		
53		
54		
55		
TOTAL	$	$
GRAND TOTAL	$	

Should amount to at least ( )%
of year's objective—both number of
sales and volume.

DEFINITIONS

Calls	Attempt to see
Finals	Actual attempt to close
Questionnaires Completed	Fact-finding forms
Service Calls	Customer
Appointments Prearranged	Telephone or otherwise
New Prospects	People you've never tried to close before or clients you haven't tried to sell for a year

13 WEEKS FORMULA FOR SUCCESS

RESOLUTION FOR THE WEEK

1. Enthusiasm
2. Order: Self-organization
3. Others
4. Questions
5. Key issue
6. Silence: Listen
7. Sincerity: Deserve confidence
8. Knowledge of my business
9. Appreciation and praise
10. Smile: Happiness
11. Remember names and faces
12. Service and prospecting
13. Closing the sale: ACTION

	MONDAY	TUESDAY	WEDNESDAY
A.M.			
LUNCH			
P.M.			

～ *Take the Resolution*

1. ENTHUSIASM . . .

Make a high and holy resolve that
thusiasm that you have been putting

To Become Enthusiastic—

—*Offer daily prayers this week*

HOW TO GET THERE!

THURSDAY	FRIDAY	SATURDAY	
			SELF-ORGANIZATION DAY Save time by following directions on Page 243. This is not the most difficult thing of all—but all the rest depends on it!
			Never leave the office until your entire week is planned ahead. Allow nothing or anybody to interfere with your Schedule. During the week you may be tempted to change some of your plans. *DON'T.* Each week you will improve in your ability to Think things through and Plan Ahead.

of the Week ~

you will double the amount of en-
into your work and into your life.

ACT Enthusiastic!

repeating these affirmations—

WEEK ENDING

RECORD OF CALLS,

KEEP THIS RECORD DAILY	Calls	Finals (Closing Int'vs.)	Appointments Pre-arranged	Questionnaires Completed	Interviews		Evenings in Field
					New	Old	
MONDAY							
TUESDAY							
WEDNESDAY							
THURSDAY							
FRIDAY							
SATURDAY							
TOTAL THIS WEEK							
PREVIOUS TOTAL							
TOTAL TO DATE							

YEAR
TO DATE

AHEAD

BEHIND

INTERVIEWS AND RESULTS

Referred New Leads	Customers: Service Calls Should be After 3 P.M.	Total Orders		Total Paid Business		Total Com- missions
		No.	Amount	No.	Amount	
			$		$	$
			$		$	$
			$		$	$
			$		$	$
			$		$	$
			$		$	$

	MONDAY	TUESDAY	WEDNESDAY
A.M.			
LUNCH			
P.M.			

⟋ Take the Resolution

2. ORDER: SELF-ORGANIZATION . . .

Let all things have their places; let each
solve to perform what you ought; per-

—Offer daily prayers this week

HOW TO GET THERE!

THURSDAY	FRIDAY	SATURDAY	
			SELF-ORGANIZATION DAY Save time by following directions on Page 243. This is not the most difficult thing of all—but all the rest depends on it!
			Never leave the office until your entire week is planned ahead. Allow nothing or anybody to interfere with your Schedule.
			During the week you may be tempted to change some of your plans. *DON'T*. Each week you will improve in your ability to Think things through and Plan Ahead.

of the Week ﹏

part of your business have its time. Reform without fail what you resolve!

repeating these affirmations—

KEEP THIS RECORD DAILY	Calls	Finals (Closing Int'vs.)	Appoint-ments Pre-arranged	Question-naires Com-pleted	Inter-views		Eve-nings in Field
					New	Old	
MONDAY							
TUESDAY							
WEDNESDAY							
THURSDAY							
FRIDAY							
SATURDAY							
TOTAL THIS WEEK							
PREVIOUS TOTAL							
TOTAL TO DATE							

YEAR
TO DATE

AHEAD

BEHIND

INTERVIEWS AND RESULTS

Referred New Leads	Customers: Service Calls Should be After 3 P.M.	Total Orders		Total Paid Business		Total Commissions
		No.	Amount	No.	Amount	
			$		$	$
		$		$	$	
		$		$	$	
		$		$	$	

$ $ $

$ $ $

WEEK BEGINNING

WHERE TO GO AND

	MONDAY	TUESDAY	WEDNESDAY
A.M.			
LUNCH			
P.M.			

∽ *Take the Resolution*

3. THINK IN TERMS OF OTHERS' INTERESTS ...

The most important secret of salesmanship is to find out what
get it.
... Help me get my mind off myself and what I am going to
what he will get out of the sale.

—*Offer daily prayers this week*

HOW TO GET THERE!

THURSDAY	FRIDAY	SATURDAY	
			SELF-ORGANIZATION DAY Save time by following directions on Page 243. This is not the most difficult thing of all—but all the rest depends on it! Never leave the office until your entire week is planned ahead. Allow nothing or anybody to interfere with your Schedule. During the week you may be tempted to change some of your plans. *DON'T*. Each week you will improve in your ability to Think things through and Plan Ahead.

of the Week ⤳

the other fellow wants, then help him find the best way to

make out of a sale, and get my mind on the other person and

repeating these affirmations—

WEEK ENDING

RECORD OF CALLS,

KEEP THIS RECORD DAILY	Calls	Finals (Closing Int'vs.)	Appoint-ments Pre-arranged	Question-naires Com-pleted	Inter-views		Eve-nings in Field
					New	Old	
MONDAY							
TUESDAY							
WEDNESDAY							
THURSDAY							
FRIDAY							
SATURDAY							
TOTAL THIS WEEK							
PREVIOUS TOTAL							
TOTAL TO DATE							

YEAR
TO DATE

AHEAD

BEHIND

———— 19—

INTERVIEWS AND RESULTS

Referred New Leads	Customers: Service Calls Should be After 3 P.M.	Total Orders		Total Paid Business		Total Com- missions
		No.	Amount	No.	Amount	
			$		$	$
			$		$	$
			$		$	$
			$		$	$

			$		$	$
			$		$	$

	MONDAY	TUESDAY	WEDNESDAY
A.M.			
LUNCH			
P.M.			

∽ Take the Resolution

4. QUESTIONS . . .

Cultivate the art of asking questions. Questions, rather than a sale, or winning people to your way of thinking. Inquire

—Offer daily prayers this week

HOW TO GET THERE!

THURSDAY	FRIDAY	SATURDAY	
			SELF- ORGANIZATION DAY Save time by follow-ing directions on Page 243. This is not the most difficult thing of all—but all the rest depends on it! Never leave the office until your entire week is planned ahead. Allow noth-ing or anybody to interfere with your Schedule. During the week you may be tempted to change some of your plans. *DON'T.* Each week you will im-prove in your ability to Think things through and Plan Ahead.

of the Week ∽

positive statements, can be the most effective means of making rather than attack.

repeating these affirmations—

WEEK ENDING

RECORD OF CALLS,

KEEP THIS RECORD DAILY	Calls	Finals (Closing Int'vs.)	Appoint-ments Pre-arranged	Question-naires Com-pleted	Inter-views		Eve-nings in Field
					New	Old	
MONDAY							
TUESDAY							
WEDNESDAY							
THURSDAY							
FRIDAY							
SATURDAY							
TOTAL THIS WEEK							
PREVIOUS TOTAL							
TOTAL TO DATE							

YEAR
TO DATE

AHEAD

BEHIND

INTERVIEWS AND RESULTS

Referred New Leads	Customers: Service Calls Should be After 3 P.M.	Total Orders		Total Paid Business		Total Commissions
		No.	Amount	No.	Amount	
			$		$	$
			$		$	$
			$		$	$
			$		$	$
			$		$	$
			$		$	$

WEEK BEGINNING

WHERE TO GO AND

	MONDAY	TUESDAY	WEDNESDAY
A.M.			
LUNCH			
P.M.			

∽ Take the Resolution

5. KEY ISSUE ...

The main problem in the sale is to:
1. Find the basic need, or
2. The main point of interest.
3. Then stick to it!

—Offer daily prayers this week

HOW TO GET THERE!

THURSDAY	FRIDAY	SATURDAY	
			SELF-ORGANIZATION DAY Save time by following directions on Page 243. This is not the most difficult thing of all—but all the rest depends on it!
			Never leave the office until your entire week is planned ahead. Allow nothing or anybody to interfere with your Schedule.
			During the week you may be tempted to change some of your plans. *DON'T.* Each week you will improve in your ability to Think things through and Plan Ahead.

of the Week ⤳

Lincoln said: "Much of my success as a trial lawyer lay in the fact that I was always willing to give the opposing attorney six points in order to gain the seventh—if the seventh was the most important."

repeating these affirmations—

WEEK ENDING

RECORD OF CALLS,

KEEP THIS RECORD DAILY	Calls	Finals (Closing Int'vs.)	Appoint- ments Pre- arranged	Question- naires Com- pleted	Inter- views		Eve- nings in Field
					New	Old	
MONDAY							
TUESDAY							
WEDNESDAY							
THURSDAY							
FRIDAY							
SATURDAY							
TOTAL THIS WEEK							
PREVIOUS TOTAL							
TOTAL TO DATE							

YEAR
TO DATE

AHEAD

BEHIND

INTERVIEWS AND RESULTS

Referred New Leads	Customers: Service Calls Should be After 3 P.M.	Total Orders		Total Paid Business		Total Com- missions
		No.	Amount	No.	Amount	
			$		$	$
			$		$	$
			$		$	$
			$		$	$

			$		$	$
			$		$	$

	MONDAY	TUESDAY	WEDNESDAY
A.M.			
LUNCH			
P.M.			

⌒ Take the Resolution

6. SILENCE. LISTEN ...

"Play 'em straight in front of you!" ... Show the other person the eager attention and appreciation that he craves and is so

—Offer daily prayers this week

HOW TO GET THERE!

THURSDAY	FRIDAY	SATURDAY	
			SELF-ORGANIZATION DAY Save time by following directions on Page 243. This is not the most difficult thing of all—but all the rest depends on it!
			Never leave the office until your entire week is planned ahead. Allow nothing or anybody to interfere with your Schedule.
			During the week you may be tempted to change some of your plans. *DON'T.* Each week you will improve in your ability to Think things through and Plan Ahead.

of the Week ᔆ

you are sincerely interested in what he is saying; give him all
hungry for, but seldom gets!

repeating these affirmations—

WEEK ENDING

RECORD OF CALLS,

KEEP THIS RECORD DAILY	Calls	Finals (Closing Int'vs.)	Appoint-ments Pre-arranged	Question-naires Com-pleted	Inter-views		Eve-nings in Field
					New	Old	
MONDAY							
TUESDAY							
WEDNESDAY							
THURSDAY							
FRIDAY							
SATURDAY							
TOTAL THIS WEEK							
PREVIOUS TOTAL							
TOTAL TO DATE							

YEAR
TO DATE

AHEAD

BEHIND

INTERVIEWS AND RESULTS

Referred New Leads	Customers: Service Calls Should be After 3 P.M.	Total Orders		Total Paid Business		Total Commissions
		No.	Amount	No.	Amount	
			$		$	$
			$		$	$
			$		$	$
			$		$	$

| | | $ | | $ | $ |
| | | $ | | $ | $ |

	MONDAY	TUESDAY	WEDNESDAY
A.M.			
LUNCH			
P.M.			

～ *Take the Resolution*

7. SINCERITY: DESERVE CONFIDENCE . . .

To win and hold the confidence of others, Rule Number
Remember the immortal words of Solomon S. Huebner: "In
rule of professional conduct: I shall in the light of all circum-
to ascertain and understand, give him that service which, had
myself."

—Offer daily prayers this week

HOW TO GET THERE!

THURSDAY	FRIDAY	SATURDAY	
			SELF-ORGANIZATION DAY Save time by following directions on Page 243. This is not the most difficult thing of all—but all the rest depends on it!
			Never leave the office until your entire week is planned ahead. Allow nothing or anybody to interfere with your Schedule. During the week you may be tempted to change some of your plans. *DON'T.* Each week you will improve in your ability to Think things through and Plan Ahead.

of the Week ⤳

One is: *Deserve Confidence!*
all my relations with clients, I agree to observe the following
stances surrounding my client, which I shall make every effort
I been in the same circumstances, I would have applied to

repeating these affirmations—

WEEK ENDING
RECORD OF CALLS.

KEEP THIS RECORD DAILY	Calls	Finals (Closing Int'vs.)	Appoint- ments Pre- arranged	Question- naires Com- pleted	Inter- views New	Inter- views Old	Eve- nings in Field
MONDAY							
TUESDAY							
WEDNESDAY							
THURSDAY							
FRIDAY							
SATURDAY							
TOTAL THIS WEEK							
PREVIOUS TOTAL							
TOTAL TO DATE							

YEAR
TO DATE

AHEAD

BEHIND

—— 19—

INTERVIEWS AND RESULTS

Referred New Leads	Customers: Service Calls Should be After 3 P.M.	Total Orders		Total Paid Business		Total Commissions
		No.	Amount	No.	Amount	
			$		$	$
			$		$	$
			$		$	$
			$		$	$
			$		$	$
			$		$	$

	MONDAY	TUESDAY	WEDNESDAY
A.M.			
LUNCH			
P.M.			

∽ *Take the Resolution*

8. KNOWLEDGE OF MY BUSINESS . . .

To have confidence in yourself, and win
essential rule is to: *Know your business*

—*Offer daily prayers this week*

HOW TO GET THERE!

THURSDAY	FRIDAY	SATURDAY	
			SELF-ORGANIZATION DAY Save time by following directions on Page 243. This is not the most difficult thing of all—but all the rest depends on it!
			Never leave the office until your entire week is planned ahead. Allow nothing or anybody to interfere with your Schedule.
			During the week you may be tempted to change some of your plans. *DON'T.* Each week you will improve in your ability to Think things through and Plan Ahead.

of the Week ∿

and hold the confidence of others, an
and keep on knowing your business.

repeating these affirmations—

WEEK ENDING

RECORD OF CALLS,

KEEP THIS RECORD DAILY	Calls	Finals (Closing Int'vs.)	Appointments Pre-arranged	Questionnaires Completed	Interviews		Evenings in Field
					New	Old	
MONDAY							
TUESDAY							
WEDNESDAY							
THURSDAY							
FRIDAY							
SATURDAY							
TOTAL THIS WEEK							
PREVIOUS TOTAL							
TOTAL TO DATE							

YEAR
TO DATE

AHEAD

BEHIND

INTERVIEWS AND RESULTS

Referred New Leads	Customers: Service Calls Should be After 3 P.M.	Total Orders		Total Paid Business		Total Commissions
		No.	Amount	No.	Amount	
			$		$	$
			$		$	$
			$		$	$
			$		$	$

		$		$	$
		$		$	$

WEEK BEGINNING

WHERE TO GO AND

	MONDAY	TUESDAY	WEDNESDAY
A.M.			
LUNCH			
P.M.			

～ *Take the Resolution*

9. APPRECIATION AND PRAISE . . .

Everyone likes to feel important. People
appreciation. Show that you believe in
If your interest is sincere, there is noth-

—Offer daily prayers this week

HOW TO GET THERE!

THURSDAY	FRIDAY	SATURDAY	
			SELF-ORGANIZATION DAY Save time by following directions on Page 243. This is not the most difficult thing of all—but all the rest depends on it!
			Never leave the office until your entire week is planned ahead. Allow nothing or anybody to interfere with your Schedule.
			During the week you may be tempted to change some of your plans. *DON'T*. Each week you will improve in your ability to Think things through and Plan Ahead.

of the Week ∽

are hungry for praise, starving for honest
them and expect bigger things of them.
ing they appreciate more.

repeating these affirmations—

RECORD OF CALLS,

KEEP THIS RECORD DAILY	Calls	Finals (Closing Int'vs.)	Appointments Pre-arranged	Questionnaires Completed	Interviews		Evenings in Field
					New	Old	
MONDAY							
TUESDAY							
WEDNESDAY							
THURSDAY							
FRIDAY							
SATURDAY							
TOTAL THIS WEEK							
PREVIOUS TOTAL							
TOTAL TO DATE							

YEAR
TO DATE

AHEAD

BEHIND

INTERVIEWS AND RESULTS

Referred New Leads	Customers: Service Calls Should be After 3 P.M.	Total Orders		Total Paid Business		Total Com- missions
		No.	Amount	No.	Amount	
			$		$	$
			$		$	$
			$		$	$
			$		$	$

		$		$		$
		$		$		$

	MONDAY	TUESDAY	WEDNESDAY
A.M.			
LUNCH			
P.M.			

∽ Take the Resolution

10. SMILE: HAPPINESS . . .

If you want to be welcome everywhere, give every living
inside, even your own wife and children—and see how much

—Offer daily prayers this week

HOW TO GET THERE!

THURSDAY	FRIDAY	SATURDAY	
			SELF-ORGANIZATION DAY Save time by following directions on Page 243. This is not the most difficult thing of all—but all the rest depends on it!
			Never leave the office until your entire week is planned ahead. Allow nothing or anybody to interfere with your Schedule.
			During the week you may be tempted to change some of your plans. *DON'T.* Each week you will improve in your ability to Think things through and Plan Ahead.

of the Week ᥐ

soul you meet an honest-to-goodness smile, from down deep
better *you* feel and look!

repeating these affirmations—

WEEK ENDING

RECORD OF CALLS,

KEEP THIS RECORD DAILY	Calls	Finals (Closing Int'vs.)	Appoint-ments Pre-arranged	Question-naires Com-pleted	Inter-views		Eve-nings in Field
					New	Old	
MONDAY							
TUESDAY							
WEDNESDAY							
THURSDAY							
FRIDAY							
SATURDAY							
TOTAL THIS WEEK							
PREVIOUS TOTAL							
TOTAL TO DATE							

YEAR
TO DATE

AHEAD

BEHIND

INTERVIEWS AND RESULTS

Referred New Leads	Customers: Service Calls Should be After 3 P.M.	Total Orders		Total Paid Business		Total Com- missions
		No.	Amount	No.	Amount	
			$		$	$
			$		$	$
			$		$	$
			$		$	$

			$		$	$
			$		$	$

	MONDAY	TUESDAY	WEDNESDAY
A.M.			
LUNCH			
P.M.			

⟿ *Take the Resolution*

11. REMEMBER NAMES AND FACES . . .

1. *Impression*—Get a clear impression of the name. Form
2. *Repetition*—Repeat the name immediately and often. peat it often enough, and at intervals.
3. *Association*—Associate a person's name with his appear- circumstances under which you met him.

—Offer daily prayers this week

HOW TO GET THERE!

THURSDAY	FRIDAY	SATURDAY	
			SELF- ORGANIZATION DAY Save time by follow-ing directions on Page 243. This is not the most difficult thing of all—but all the rest depends on it!
			Never leave the office until your entire week is planned ahead. Allow noth-ing or anybody to interfere with your Schedule. During the week you may be tempted to change some of your plans. *DON'T*. Each week you will im-prove in your ability to Think things through and Plan Ahead.

of the Week ～

the habit of taking a mental photograph of the name.
You can remember almost anything if you will only re-

ance, or business. Try to get an action picture of the

repeating these affirmations—

KEEP THIS RECORD DAILY	Calls	Finals (Closing Int'vs.)	Appoint-ments Pre-arranged	Question-naires Com-pleted	Inter-views		Eve-nings in Field
					New	Old	
MONDAY							
TUESDAY							
WEDNESDAY							
THURSDAY							
FRIDAY							
SATURDAY							
TOTAL THIS WEEK							
PREVIOUS TOTAL							
TOTAL TO DATE							

YEAR
TO DATE

AHEAD

BEHIND

———— 19—

INTERVIEWS AND RESULTS

Referred New Leads	Customers: Service Calls Should be After 3 P.M.	Total Orders		Total Paid Business		Total Com- missions
		No.	Amount	No.	Amount	
			$		$	$
			$		$	$
			$		$	$
			$		$	$

		$			$	$
		$			$	$

WEEK BEGINNING

WHERE TO GO AND

	MONDAY	TUESDAY	WEDNESDAY
A.M.			
LUNCH			
P.M.			

∽ *Take the Resolution*

12. SERVICE AND PROSPECTING . . .

1. "Never forget a customer—Never let
2. New customers are the best source
3. Never let a sale run into a dead end.

—Offer daily prayers this week

HOW TO GET THERE!

THURSDAY	FRIDAY	SATURDAY	
			SELF-ORGANIZATION DAY Save time by following directions on Page 243. This is not the most difficult thing of all—but all the rest depends on it! Never leave the office until your entire week is planned ahead. Allow nothing or anybody to interfere with your Schedule. During the week you may be tempted to change some of your plans. *DON'T.* Each week you will improve in your ability to Think things through and Plan Ahead.

of the Week ⌇

a customer forget you."
of new business . . . *new* customers!
"Play position for the next shot!"

repeating these affirmations—

WEEK ENDING

RECORD OF CALLS,

KEEP THIS RECORD DAILY	Calls	Finals (Closing Int'vs.)	Appoint- ments Pre- arranged	Question- naires Com- pleted	Inter- views		Eve- nings in Field
					New	Old	
MONDAY							
TUESDAY							
WEDNESDAY							
THURSDAY							
FRIDAY							
SATURDAY							
TOTAL THIS WEEK							
PREVIOUS TOTAL							
TOTAL TO DATE							

YEAR
TO DATE

AHEAD

BEHIND

INTERVIEWS AND RESULTS

Referred New Leads	Customers: Service Calls Should be After 3 P.M.	Total Orders		Total Paid Business		Total Com-missions
		No.	Amount	No.	Amount	
			$		$	$
			$		$	$
			$		$	$
			$		$	$

			$		$	$
			$		$	$

	MONDAY	TUESDAY	WEDNESDAY
A.M.			
LUNCH			
P.M.			

∾ *Take the Resolution*

13. CLOSING THE SALE: ACTION!

1. Just before going into a man's office, repeat these words *had!*

2. "You never know what's in a man's mind by what he tions, he doesn't mean he won't buy. What he *really* produced enough evidence to make him *want* to buy!

   —*Offer daily prayers this week*

HOW TO GET THERE!

THURSDAY	FRIDAY	SATURDAY	
			SELF-ORGANIZATION DAY Save time by following directions on Page 243. This is not the most difficult thing of all—but all the rest depends on it!
			Never leave the office until your entire week is planned ahead. Allow nothing or anybody to interfere with your Schedule.
			During the week you may be tempted to change some of your plans. *DON'T.* Each week you will improve in your ability to Think things through and Plan Ahead.

of the Week ～

to yourself: *This is going to be the best interview I ever*

says." Welcome objections! When a man offers objec-
means is that you haven't convinced him yet. You haven't

repeating these affirmations—

WEEK ENDING

RECORD OF CALLS,

KEEP THIS RECORD DAILY	Calls	Finals (Closing Int'vs.)	Appoint-ments Pre-arranged	Question-naires Com-pleted	Inter-views		Eve-nings in Field
					New	Old	
MONDAY							
TUESDAY							
WEDNESDAY							
THURSDAY							
FRIDAY							
SATURDAY							
TOTAL THIS WEEK							
PREVIOUS TOTAL							
TOTAL TO DATE							

YEAR
TO DATE

AHEAD

BEHIND

INTERVIEWS AND RESULTS

Referred New Leads	Customers: Service Calls Should be After 3 P.M.	Total Orders		Total Paid Business		Total Commissions
		No.	Amount	No.	Amount	
			$		$	$
			$		$	$
			$		$	$
			$		$	$
			$		$	$
			$		$	$

NEW LEADS OBTAINED

To Insure Consistent Production Secure on Average
( ) Qualified Names Daily—( ) WEEKLY

NAME	REFERRED BY:	
	Name	Reported Results

TRANSFER EACH NAME TO A PROSPECT CARD DAILY

NEW LEADS OBTAINED

To Insure Consistent Production Secure on Average
( ) Qualified Names Daily—( ) WEEKLY

NAME	REFERRED BY:	
	Name	Reported Results

TRANSFER EACH NAME TO A PROSPECT CARD DAILY

NEW LEADS OBTAINED

To Insure Consistent Production Secure on Average
( ) Qualified Names Daily—( ) WEEKLY

NAME	REFERRED BY:	
	Name	Reported Results

TRANSFER EACH NAME TO A PROSPECT CARD DAILY

NEW LEADS OBTAINED

To Insure Consistent Production Secure on Average
( ) Qualified Names Daily–( ) WEEKLY

NAME	REFERRED BY:	
	Name	Reported Results

TRANSFER EACH NAME TO A PROSPECT CARD DAILY

RESULTS
13 WEEKS SUBMITTED BUSINESS

Name	Amount	Name	Amount
		13 Weeks	$
		Previous Total	$
		Year to Date	$

ANALYZER

You Can Get More Inspiration Out of Studying Your
Own Records Than From Any Other Source

COMPARE WITH PREVIOUS RECORDS

1. Commission Value Each Closing Interview?
2. Amount Paid Business Per Closing Interview?
3. Number of Closing Interviews Per Sale?
4. Sales on First Closing Interview?
5. "   " Second "   "   ?
6. "   " Third and Later "   ?
7. Did I Ask for Names on Each Call—Sale or No Sale?
   (Did I Report Results, Good or Bad, Promptly to
   Friends?)
8. How Many Completed Questionnaires Did I Average Per
   Week?
9. How Many Old Customers Did I Sell?
10. Resolution of the Week: Did I Try to Follow Benjamin
    Franklin's Example?
    Did I Pray About It?

Insure Your Success

If your results are not satisfactory, study
your records. You'll find the real reason.

Don't Be Afraid to Fail

Keep working at it. Each week, each month, you'll improve.
Tomorrow, you will find a way to do the thing that today looks
impossible. With this plan, you can maintain your enthusiasm
. . . *and I believe if a man can maintain enthusiasm long
enough, it will produce anything!*

FRANKLIN WROTE: "... and conceiving God to be the fountain of wisdom, I thought it right and necessary to solicit His assistance for obtaining it; to this end, I formed the following prayer which was prefixed to my tables of examination for daily use."

Here is the prayer—Ben Franklin's prayer:

O powerful Goodness! bountiful Father! merciful Guide! Increase in me that wisdom which discovers my truest interest. Strengthen my resolutions to perform what that wisdom dictates. Accept my kind offices to Thy other children as the only return in my power for Thy continual favors to me.

Appendix A
CLOSE CORPORATION
(Confidential Information)

Name: _____

In which state incorporated and date: _____

Capital stock authorized: Common $ _____

Preferred $ _____

Capital stock issued: Common $ _____

Preferred $ _____

Rate of interest on preferred: _____

If interest on preferred is passed, does it become voting? _____

Terms for retirement of preferred stock: _____

Common stockholders: names, ages, heirs, minor children, number of shares held by each shareholder, active in the business or inactive:

_____

_____

_____

_____

_____

Sons active in the business: _____

_____

Average payroll: _____

Present value per share of common stock not counting good will: _____

Existing stock purchase agreement in the event of death? _____

date: _____

Existing life insurance owned by corporation on lives of officers: _____

Key man insurance: _____

Purpose of the life insurance: _____

Who pays premiums: _____

Real estate, securities, cash on hand, other assets: _____

_____

Mortgage, notes, other obligations; any notes or obligations endorsed by individuals: _____

_____

Salaries of officers: _____

Appendix B

PARTNERSHIP

(Confidential Information)

Name of firm: _____

Names of each partner, share of interest in the firm, ages, health, heirs, minor children. Is each partner active in the business? _____

_____

_____

_____

_____

_____

Terms of agreement: _____

_____

Provisions of agreement in event of death of a partner: _____

_____

_____ binding or optional? _____

Present value of partnership: $____Value of good will?____

Existing partnership life insurance: _____

Key man insurance: _____

Purpose of the life insurance: _____

Real estate, securities, cash on hand, other assets: _____

_____

Mortgage, notes, other obligations: _____

_____

Salaries of partners: _____

_____

Index

A

Absolute contract of sale, 162
"Acres of Diamonds" (Russell Conwell), 148-149, 220
Action:
  closing the sale, 247, 272-273
  need for, 9-10
Agents, life insurance:
  code of, 96
  insurance on own lives, 119-121
  relations with company, 86-88
Allen, William F., 109-111
Analysis:
  estate, 62
  personal estate, 49-54
  of records, 28, 305
  of use of questions, 192-194
Analyzer, 305-306
Annuities, 129-131, 145
  nonattachability of, 132
Application for life insurance, getting check with, 134-137
Appointments:
  prearranged, 247
  secret of making, 193-194
  selling, 194
Appreciation of others, 247, 264-265
Approach, 37-41
  critical moment for, 194
  front-door, 38
  importance of, 37
  model for, 37
  talk, 38-41
  two-interview system, 41
Artel, Jorge, 142
Association, and remembering, 268-269
Autobiography of Benjamin Franklin, The, 233

B

Balance Sheet, 46-47, 48, 63
Baldwin, Matthias William, 172
Baldwin Locomotive Works, 169-173
Bankrupt, insurance of, 213-214
"Bowers, John," 59-65
Bresnahan, Roger, 69-70
Brown, Floyd, 119
Brush-off talk, 196
Business perpetuation plans, 178-180, 186-188
Buy-and-sell agreement funded with life insurance, 189
Buying signals, 55, 56
  objections as, 82-85

C

Calls:
  dollars and cents value of, 225-226
  record of, 274-299
  service, 247
  step diagram of, 230
Campbell, Richard W., 17, 41, 232
Canned sales talks, 41
Cantrell, George, letter from, 145
Capital, amount needed, defined, 247
Cards:
  birthday, 26
  of introduction, 22-23, 24, 93
  prospect, 300-303
Carnegie, Dale, 235
  courses in public speaking, 206, 214-215
  letter from, 143-144
Chartered Life Underwriters, American College of, code of, 96
Close corporations, 164

Close corporations (*cont.*):
 confidential information, form, 307
Closing the sale, 37, 247, 272-273
 getting check with application, 134-137
 "holding on longer," 58
 magic phrase, 117
 story-telling in, 125-127
Cobb, Ty, 19-20
Code of C.L.U., 96
Collings, Karl, 19, 99
Commissions, splitting, 156
Company, life insurance on president of, 175-181
Competition, 12
Confidence:
 deserving, 247, 260-261
 in self, 262-263
Connor, Jim, 120
Connor-Taylor sale, 183-194
 analysis of, 192-194
Contract of sale, absolute, 162
Conversation, with leads, 23-25
Conwell, Russell, 148-149, 220
Corporation insurance, 174-182
 life insurance on president, 176-181
Courage, developing, 206-207
Credit:
 helping prospects to obtain, 79-81
 increased by life insurance, 110-111
Creditors, reduction of their losses, 213-214
Customers, new, 21

D

Daily record, form, 274-299
Dead end salesmanship, 20, 26, 29, 270, 271
Death of partner, 186
Definitions, 247
Depression, 76
 salesmanship during, 31-33
 as strait jacket, 82

Dewey, John, 235
Doolin, Lawrence J. 16-17
Down the Fairway (Bobby Jones), 14

E

Early rising, importance of, 12
Edison, Thomas A., 172
Emerson, Ralph Waldo, quoted, 101
Enid, Oklahoma, sales clinic in, 37-38
Enthusiasm, 166, 247, 248-249
 maintenance of, 12
 principle of, 234
Estate analysis, 62
Excuses of prospects:
 brush-off talk, 196
 don't believe in life insurance, 59-69
 no money, 182, 218
 not interested, 185
 too busy, 70
 too old, 183

F

Faces, remembering, 247, 268-269
Failure, fear of, 305
Family maintenance rider, 53, 141
Family record, 50
Fear:
 conquest of, 206-207
 effect of, story, 229-231
 of failure, 305
 rules for conquering, 166-167
Fidelity Mutual Life Insurance Company, 3
Finals, defined, 247
Forms:
 confidential information:
  close corporation, 307
  partnership, 308
 daily record, 274-299
 new leads obtained, 300-303
 personal estate analysis, 49-54

Forms (*cont.*):
  personal estate inventory, 44-46
  13 weeks submitted business, 304
Franklin, Benjamin, 235
  Autobiography of, 233
  Junto, 207
  on partnerships, 205
  prayer of, 306
  quoted, 12, 178
From Failure to Success in Selling
  (Bettger), 38
Fuller Brush salesmen, 13

G

Go-getter *vs.* Go-giver, 215
Gough, Austin, 32
Gould, Al, 31-33
Graham, Sara, 221
Green, Robert M., 168

H

Hagen, Fred, 19
Hall, J. Elliott, 69
Hamlin, Clay, 232
Happiness, 247, 266-267
High-pressure salesmanship, 58
  getting check with application,
    135
Hobbies of prospects, 42-43, 61
Hodge, Charles G., 3
Howard, Jack, 82, 83
Huebner, Solomon S., 96
  quoted, 272
Hunsicker, Clayton M., 95-96, 125-
    126, 155-160
Husband and wife:
  partnership, 201-202
  young, insurance for, 138-141

I

I.B.M.'s *Weekly Work Sheet*, 13
Inheritance taxes, 202, 217
Inspiration, 203-204

Interests of clients:
  servicing, 25-26
  thinking in terms of, 247, 252-253
Interview, 48-55
  fact-finding (*see* Questionnaire)
  first, 247
  magic phrases, 56
  prearranged, 247
  record of interviews, 274-299
  two-interview system, 41
Introduction, letters and cards of,
    22-23, 93
Inventory:
  of new prospects, 244-245
  of old prospects, 246
Isman, Felix, story of, 132-133

J

"Jones, Bill," story of, 229-232
Jones, Bobby, quoted, 14
Junto speaking experiences, 207

K

Kansas City, Mo., sales clinic in, 126
Kelly, George, 1-2, 8
Key issue in sale, 247, 256-257
Key man:
  insured by company, 196-197
  stock sold to, 202
  locating, 195-197
Koehler, Robert P., 212, 223
Krauss, Henry, story of, 198-204
Kroll, Ray, 198

L

Laughter, 217
Leads:
  asking for, 23-25, 26
  magic phrases that produce, 29
  new, 15, 16, 20
  showing appreciation for, 25-26,
    29-30
Lee, Ivy, 9-10

Leibowitz, Samuel S., 46
Letters of introduction, 22-23
Life insurance:
 borrowing on, 175
 buy-and-sell agreement funded
  with, 189
 relations with agents, 86-88
 joint selling of, 156
 kinds of, 139-141
 "short course in," 139-141
 steps in taking out, 164-165
 salesmanship, 3
  Y.M.C.A. courses in, 211-214
Life Underwriters, National Quality
 Award for, 16
Lincoln, Abraham, quoted, 256
Listening, value of, 247, 258-259
Loans, protected with life insurance,
 222-223

M

McGraw, John, 70
Magic phrases, 101, 114, 182
 corporation insurance, 182
 deal before deal, 92
 rated policies, 107
 that produce names and leads, 29
Mailing pieces, 26
Memorized sales talks, 41
Miller, Charley, 2
Million Dollar Round Table, 232
Monthly mailing piece, 26
Mortgage, liquidation of, 202
Moss, Ralph, 4
Moss, Warren, 4

N

Names (see also Leads):
 magic phrases that produce, 29
 remembering, aids in, 268-269
National Quality Award for Life
 Underwriters, 16
New customers, 21, 270, 271

New leads, form for recording, 303
New prospects, 15, 16, 17, 198
 card file for, 300-303
 defined, 247
 inventory of, 244-245
Niemeyer, Dean, 37-38

O

Objections of prospects, 192
 as buying signals, 82-85
 welcoming, 272, 273
Oliver, John, 125
Oppenheimer, Mr., 20-21
Orderliness, value of, 247, 250-251
Ordinary life policy, 139, 140-141
Orr, Millard, 152
Ownership management plan, 178,
 180, 186-188

P

Paret, Louis, 234-235
Partners:
 death of partner, 186
  one or more, rejected, 108-113
 selling to, 108-113, 115-117
Partnership insurance, 135, 157-165,
 180, 183-194
 Baldwin Locomotive Works, 169,
  170
 confidential information form,
  308
 Connor-Taylor sale, 183-194
 husband and wife, 201-202
 John Haines story, 157-159, 161
 steps in taking out, 164-165, 167
Partnerships, B. Franklin on, 205
Patterson, Judge, 162-164
Personal estate analysis, 48-53
Personal estate inventory, 44-46
Philadelphia Life Underwriters'
 Association, speech before
 luncheon meeting, 234-235
Physical examination, 164, 178

Planning and plans (*see also* 13 weeks formula for success) :
business perpetuation plan, 178-180, 186-188
day-to-day *vs.* all day, 11
four steps, 164-165, 167, 179-180, 191
Pocock, J. J., 21-22
Policies, rated, 102-107
Powell, Richard, 125-126
Praise, sincere, 247, 264-265
Prayer, 12
Franklin's, 306
"Preferred" rating, 87
Presentation, memorized, 41
President of company, life insurance on, 175-181
Production records (*see* Records)
Professional conduct, code of, 96
Prospecting, 19, 29, 247, 270-271
Prospects:
excuses of (*see* Excuses of prospects)
finding and supplying what they want, 75-81
getting signatures of, 66
giving valuable ideas to, 89-92
helping, to establish credit, 79-81
hobbies of, 42-43, 61
new (*see* New prospects)
old, inventory of, 246
weight reduction by, 103-105
who refuse to look at salesman, 70
Provident Mutual Life Insurance Company, speech before meeting of, 235
Public speaking, study of, 206-207, 214-215

Q

Questionnaire, 42-46, 184
questions leading to, 61
Questions:
analysis of use of, 192-194
art of asking, 247, 254-255
use of, 59-65

R

Rated policies:
delivering, 102-107
magic phrases, 107
Ratings given by life insurance companies, 87
Reader's Digest, stories in, 142
Records:
analysis of, 28, 305
comparison of, 305
daily, form, 274-299
of new leads obtained, 300-303
study of, 14-15, 16-17, 28
value of, 17-18, 232
Rehearsal, value of, 41
Reis, Henry W., Jr., 12-13
Remembering names and faces, 247, 268-269
Repeat sales, 25
Repetition, and remembering, 268-269

S

Sales, absolute contract of, 162
Sales talks:
memorized, 41
none over telephone, 194
use of "you" in, 68-69
Schmidt, Edward A., story of, 216-220
Schmidt, Harry, 5-6, 175-181
Schwab, Charles, 9-10
Scott, John, story of, 128-131
Scott, Tom, 19-20, 21, 28-29
Self-confidence, developing, 206-207
Self-organization, principle of, 234
Self-Organization Day, 11, 28, 46, 231, 243, 250-251
Selling interview, 48-53 (*see also* Interview, selling)
Selling process, 37-72 (*see also under separate headings*):
approach, 37-41
closing the sale, 57-58
interview, 48-56
preparation for, 42-47
sales talk, using questions, 59-69

Service calls, 247
Services, 247, 270-271
Shingle, Lester H., 225
Signature of prospect, 66
Sincerity, 247, 260-261
Six O'Clock Club, 12
Smiling, 247, 266-267
Speaking, public, study of, 206, 207, 214-215
Stephans, Arthur L., letter from, 224
Story-telling:
  Hunsicker on, 156
  kind of story, 126-127
  learning, 166-167
  selling as, 150
  value of, 125
Strathmann, Henry R., 214, 222-223
"Substandard" file, 106
Success:
  insuring, 305
  13 weeks formula for, 247-273 (see 13 weeks formula for success)

T

Talbot, Walter LeMar, 8-9
Telephone:
  no sales talk over, 194
  use of, 11, 247
  "witnesses" on, 146-147
Temple University, 148-149
Term insurance, 140
13 weeks formula for success, 247-273
  appreciation and praise, 247, 264-265
  closing the sale-action, 247, 272-273
  enthusiasm, 247, 248-249
  key issue in sale, 247, 256-257
  knowledge of business, 247, 262-263
  listening to prospect, 247, 258-259
  order—self-organization, 247, 250-251
  others' interests, thinking in terms of, 247, 252-253

13 weeks formula for success (cont.):
  questions, use of, 247, 254-255
  resolutions listed, 247
  service and prospecting, 247, 270-271
  sincerity — deserving confidence, 247, 260-261
  smiling—happiness, 247, 266-267
13 Weeks' Self-Organizer, 12, 13, 234, 239-273
  definitions, 247
  directions for using, 240-241
  inventory of:
    new prospects, 244-245
    old prospects, 246
  master schedule, 243
  Self-Organization Day, 243
  weekly objective, 242
13 weeks submitted business, form for results, 304
Travelers Insurance Company, 111-113
Tull, R. F., 86-87
Twenty Payment Life, 94, 95, 97, 112, 140, 141
Twenty Year Endowment, 140, 141
Two-interview system, 41

V

Vauclain, Samuel, story of, 169-173

W

Walker, William C., 57-58, 192
Weber, Gustav, 212-214, 223
Weekly objective, 242
Weekly Work Sheet, I.B.M.'s, 13
Weight of prospect, reduction of, 103-105
West, Nelson, 213, 221
Whole life policy, 139
Widows, children, and executors, 158-160, 161-163, 186, 187, 197
Wife:
  and minor children as stock owners, 175, 197

Wife (*cont.*):
    name of, on family record, 44, 45, 48-52
Wills:
    disposal of partnership interest in, 187
    recommendations concerning, 52
Wolf, Charles R., 108-113

Y

Y.M.C.A. courses in life insurance salesmanship, 211-214, 223-224
"You" and "yours," use of, 68-69
Young husbands and wives, selling to, 138-141